Antigua
and Barbuda

The heart of the Caribbean

Third Edition

Brian Dyde

CARIBBEAN

First edition 1986
Second edition 1993
Third edition 1999
Published by
MACMILLAN EDUCATION LTD
London and Basingstoke
Companies and representatives throughout the world

ISBN 0-333-74988-X

10   9   8   7   6   5   4   3   2   1
08   07   06   05   04   03   02   01   00   99

This book is printed on paper suitable for recycling and
made from fully managed and sustained forest sources.

Printed in Hong Kong

A catalogue record for this book is available from the
British Library.

Cover photographs courtesy of Chris Huxley

To   T.G.J. Joseph,
      my tutor in the university of Antigua

Contents

| Maps |

Preface to the Third Edition

When the First Edition of this book was being written at the beginning of 1985 the rate at which the Antiguan way of life was changing, and the changes which were being made to the face of the island – occasioned by a building boom which by then had been in evidence for at least five years – threatened to prevent its ever being completed. By the time it was published many of its observations were no longer true, and most of the statistics quoted were already outdated.

Although it was possible with each reprinting to get rid of the worst errors, and to take some account of what often seemed to be overnight changes in the landscape, by the beginning of the 1990s it was apparent that much of the text required a thorough overhaul, and a Second Edition was published in 1993. Although this described an island which differed in many respects from that depicted in the original edition, again, within a very short space of time, it became obvious that this also was more of a fleeting snapshot than an enduring portrait.

The completely revised Third Edition, then, is an attempt to produce a reliable and authentic portrayal of Antigua and Barbuda as the State appears in the closing years of the twentieth century; and one which it is hoped will remain valid, for a year or two at least, of the new millennium.

Meanwhile, although the pace of development (not, regrettably, all to the good or to everyone's liking) shows no signs of abating, and the face of Antigua in particular will keep on changing, the warmth and friendliness of the people of Antigua and Barbuda (for whom it is a case of *plus ça change...*) remain unaffected – the true beating of the heart of the Caribbean.

Brian Dyde
Pembroke
March 1998

Foreword

Antigua and Barbuda are two small islands about twenty-seven miles apart in the eastern Caribbean. The great majority of Antiguans have never seen let alone visited Barbuda, and it is still possible that one or two Barbudans have never been to Antigua. The State however is made up of *three* islands – the third being called Redonda, a much smaller island about thirty miles to the south-west of Antigua. Redonda can be seen clearly from Antigua on most days, but is invisible from Barbuda; it is rarely visited by anyone, having been deserted for the past sixty years or so.

I believe this rather unusual state of affairs with regard to the composition of a single country illustrates something of the individuality and independent outlook of the people of both Antigua and Barbuda. At the same time it provides a good example of an irrational State, created as a result of decisions reached merely to achieve administrative tidiness in the colonial past. Barbuda was annexed to Antigua in 1860 as a way out of intractable problems concerned with the administration of the former, and to try to stabilise the relationship between the inhabitants of the two islands. Redonda, which is considerably closer to both Montserrat and Nevis than to Antigua, was annexed in 1869 only because Antigua was then the administrative centre for the whole of the Leeward Islands Colony. Had the seat of government for this colony been in, say, St Kitts at this time it is most unlikely that either Barbuda or Redonda would now have any connection with Antigua.

I became aware while carrying out research for this book that a number of myths and quite false impressions concerning all three islands have entered folklore, which are repeated and embellished in travel books, newspaper articles and endless tourist literature. These possibly arise from the way the State was formed. Local readers must be prepared to discover that some cherished 'facts' and statistics concerning their country have little basis in truth. Who, after all, ever carried out a survey and counted one beach in Antigua for every day of the year, or found an archaeologist prepared to give credence to the erection of 'megaliths' on Green Castle Hill? My exposure of some of these myths should offend no one; Antigua and Barbuda have more than enough to offer visitors without the need to dress up their appeal with fables and half-truths.

Because of the large disparity in development, resources and population between the two islands, inevitably this book must be primarily a guide to Antigua. Barbuda, which has a unique history and offers fewer but very different attractions from those of Antigua, is the subject of one chapter, together with a brief description of Redonda. While recognising that Barbudans are proud of their island and very conscious of their individuality, if awkward syntax is to be avoided any general comments about Antiguans which follow must be taken to apply equally to citizens of both islands.

Part 1

Background

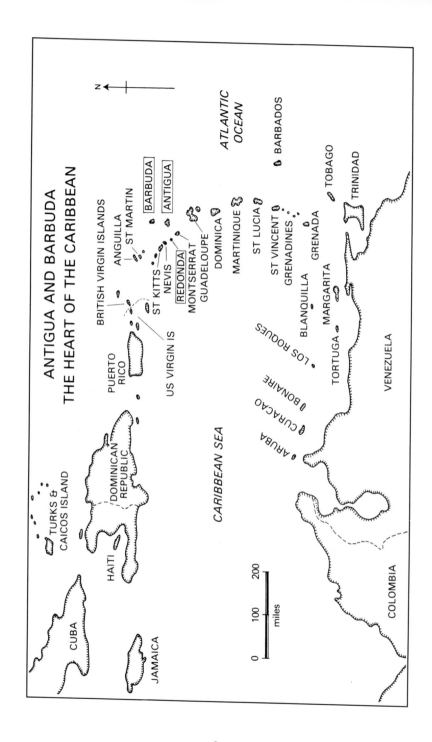

ANTIGUA AND BARBUDA
THE HEART OF THE CARIBBEAN

N

ATLANTIC OCEAN

BRITISH VIRGIN ISLANDS

ANGUILLA
ST MARTIN

BARBUDA
ANTIGUA

ST KITTS
NEVIS
REDONDA
MONTSERRAT
GUADELOUPE
DOMINICA
MARTINIQUE
ST LUCIA
ST VINCENT
GRENADINES
GRENADA

BARBADOS

TOBAGO
TRINIDAD

PUERTO RICO

US VIRGIN IS

TURKS &
CAICOS ISLAND

DOMINICAN REPUBLIC

HAITI

CUBA

JAMAICA

CARIBBEAN SEA

LOS ROQUES
BONAIRE
CURACAO
ARUBA

BLANQUILLA
TORTUGA
MARGARITA

VENEZUELA

COLOMBIA

0   100   200
miles

2

| 1 |
Introduction

Antigua – 'the heart of the Caribbean'. Can this really be so? If we consider Antigua's place in the huge arc of islands stretching from the southern tip of Florida to the coast of Venezuela, then the answer must be 'no'. But there are many 'Caribbeans': are we talking about the *geographer's* Caribbean, the *political* Caribbean, the *English-speaking* Caribbean, the *tourists'* Caribbean, or what? For most of the population of Antigua the Caribbean consists of those islands between Puerto Rico in the north-west and Trinidad in the south. For the majority of English-speaking visitors, I would suggest that, if we exclude Jamaica and the Bahamas, the same definition applies.

It is not the purpose of this book to try to prove that Antigua is in fact at the heart or hub of the Caribbean, but to provide a general view of the island and its people from which readers may draw their own conclusions. However, it is impossible to write about Antigua without stressing the importance of its location and natural facilities. Nor is it possible to write about the Antiguan people and their recent history without showing that their endeavours and achievements have reached a level far ahead of that found in many other islands in the region. By virtue of her geographical position and the continuing development of her human and natural resources it will be seen, I hope, that Antigua has a just claim to be considered as 'the heart of the Caribbean'.

This assertion is made in many of the tourist brochures, together with claims that Antigua is 'a holiday haven', 'a tourist paradise', and a place 'where land and sea make beauty'. The island does have much to offer the tourist and vacationer – indeed its economy depends on this fact – but there is much more than 'a land of perpetual sunshine' peopled by the shadowy adjuncts to the 'perfect vacation' of travel agents and tour operators. For the ordinary Antiguan the real island lies, literally, behind the beaches, the hotels and all the vacation pastimes involving sea, sun, rum punches and steel bands.

Coco Point Beach, Barbuda (overleaf) (CHRIS HUXLEY)

Other than a multitude of superb beaches, Antigua has a limited number of 'sights' and 'tourist attractions'. The majority could easily be seen in no more than a couple of days by those visitors who are interested only in places and not in people.

It is the Antiguan people themselves that make Antigua what it is. They are not there as human ornamentation of the 'sights', nor are they waiting to be pitied for the all too obvious signs of poverty here and there in the island. They are a people who have only just become possessors of their own country (the final vestiges of colonial rule disappeared as recently as 1981), and they are now busy trying to create a true nation. The island lives up to all the purple prose of the tourist brochures, but this forms only a facade – behind which the visitor can find the true and more rewarding Antigua.

Children's Carnival (CHRIS HUXLEY)

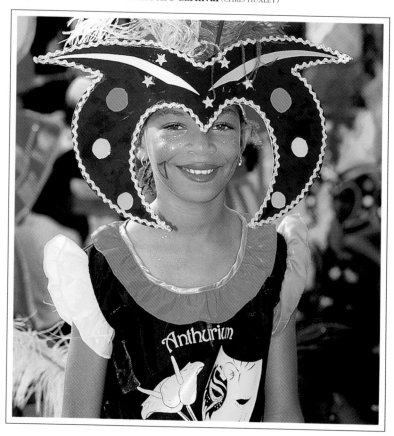

Throughout the English-speaking West Indies there is an accepted code of greeting which is widely observed. The basic rule is that the person arriving – the visitor to a house, the customer in a shop, the client entering an office – is the one who makes the opening remark. While in other parts of the world it may be unimportant who greets whom, or who speaks first, this is not so in Antigua. As with a private visitor to a house so it is with a visitor to Antigua. In very general terms you, the visitor, are expected to open any dialogue. The Antiguan is here already, you are entering his country, so common politeness means that you should acknowledge the relationship. Countless visitors have discovered that a 'Good morning', delivered at the right time and with the proper intonation, has opened up a new and far richer view of Antigua and Antiguan society. Antiguans are naturally friendly, polite and helpful, but only towards those who are prepared to show that they are well-disposed and wish to be friendly. Inevitably some visitors will find fault – the poor state of the roads, perhaps, or undue surliness in a petty official. While not in any way seeking to excuse the absence of any of the niceties of life or social behaviour, I feel it may be worthwhile for anyone made conscious of such shortcomings to reflect on one or two aspects of Antiguan history.

In terms of European settlement Antigua is as old as the USA. The first English settlers arrived in the island only twelve years after the *Mayflower* brought the Pilgrim Fathers to New England. After that, while the history of the USA shows constant change combined with the development of its resources and the advancement of its people, the same cannot be said of its tiny neighbour in the Caribbean. Under British colonial rule very little of interest to the outside world – other than the introduction and subsequent abolition of slavery – occurred in Antigua from the first settlement until well into the present century. This is shown only too clearly by the very limited amount written about the history of the island before the outbreak of the Second World War. In 1844 an anonymous author, now believed to have been a Mrs Lanaghan (or possibly Lenaghan, or even Flannigan) published a two-volume 'full account of the colony and its inhabitants from the time of the Caribs to the present day'. *Antigua and the Antiguans* is an enlightening and very readable book (as will be seen I hope from the extracts quoted hereafter), but only about half of one volume is concerned with the history of the island; the remainder being devoted to observations on its appearance, natural history, and the social life of its inhabitants, both black and white. But even this amount of history is considerably more than that found in another book published in 1894, which claimed to be *The History of the Island of Antigua*. This is a work in three enormous volumes written by Vere Langford Oliver, consisting of nothing more than a colossal list of the pedigrees of the white Antiguan proprietary families, with an insignificant amount of historical detail concerning Antigua.

The modern history of the island can be said to have begun in 1939, when the struggle to end colonial rule started in earnest just as the Second World War broke out. Within two years the circumstances of war brought US servicemen and civilian contractors to Antigua in large numbers. Thereafter, as Antiguans continued along the road to independence from Great Britain, their fortunes became more and more involved with those of North America. The influence of the USA, and later Canada, increased as the dominance of Great Britain in Antiguan affairs slowly waned and eventually disappeared. Today, with the British influence on the social and cultural life remaining as strong as ever, but with the State steadily increasing its economic ties with North America, Antigua is nicely balanced between the Old and New Worlds.

The significance of the major events in Antigua's history which have taken place within the past fifty years cannot be over-stressed. Full adult suffrage was granted only in 1951; genuine internal self-government came about in 1967, and complete independence in 1981. Few Antiguans would advance any of these facts as excuses for any inadequacy in sociability or social amenities. Despite this, the visitor with a genuine interest in Antigua and her people can only benefit from keeping them in mind.

ANTIGUA

0 1 2 3 4
miles

N

ATLANTIC OCEAN

CARIBBEAN SEA

SANDY ISLAND

LONG ISLAND

GUIANA ISLAND

GREEN ISLAND

Boon Point

St John's Harbour

Deep Bay

Five Islands Harbour

Pearns Point

Lignumvitae Bay

Johnsons Point

THE FLASHES

CEDAR GROVE

AIRPORT

ST JOHN'S

POTTERS

JENNINGS

BOLANS

EMANUEL

Boggy Peak
1319 ft

SHEKERLEY MOUNTAINS

URLINGS

Carlisle Bay

OLD ROAD

SWETES

SEA VIEW FARM

ALL SAINTS

Parham Harbour

PARHAM

PARES

POTWORKS DAM

WILLIKIES

Indian Town Point

Nonsuch Bay

NEWFIELD

FREETOWN

Half Moon Bay

BETHESDA

LIBERTA

FALMOUTH

Falmouth Harbour

English Harbour

ENGLISH HARBOUR TOWN

Willoughby Bay

Nanton Point

| 2 |
The island

Location and formation

Antigua is in the middle of the Leeward Islands which form the most northerly group of the Lesser Antilles. It is about 450 miles to the east of Hispaniola and the same distance to the north of Trinidad. Unlike most of the islands which form the eastern boundary of the Caribbean Sea it is not of volcanic origin. Instead it is formed of mainly sedimentary rocks, chiefly limestone, with the remains of very ancient volcanic activity in one corner of the island only. It sits on the southern edge of a large bank of relatively shallow water about 1200 square miles in area, with Barbuda at the northern end. With an area of about 108 square miles Antigua is very roughly oval in shape. The coastline is so irregular though, with deep bays and creeks, that to compare the island with any regular shape must stretch the imagination. There are a number of small islets close offshore, together with large areas of reefs and shoals. These reefs have made the approaches from seaward difficult throughout Antigua's history. At the same time they provide excellent protection for many of the bays, and the island has always had a reputation for possessing some of the best harbours in the West Indies.

Antigua can be divided into three main regions. The area to the south and west of a line drawn from Five Islands Harbour on the west coast to Falmouth Harbour on the south coast is the highest part. It consists of steep hills of volcanic formation, several of which are over 1000 feet in height. The highest point in the island, called Boggy Peak, is only just over 1300 feet high. The hills are covered with green vegetation, and this has given rise to the impression that they contain a tropical rain forest. In fact there are no forests of any kind in Antigua. The area also contains many steep-sided valleys which in wet weather hold fast-flowing streams. This again could give a misleading impression as there are no permanent rivers or streams in this or any other part of the island.

Darkwood Pond – birds and sugar mill (opposite) (CHRIS HUXLEY)

The central part of Antigua is an undulating plain about three miles wide, which runs diagonally across the island from St John's Harbour in the north-west to Willoughby Bay in the south-east. The boundary between this plain and the higher, more hilly country to the north is marked by a very broken limestone escarpment. This is steep in places and can be readily identified to the north of St John's, and more so where it forms the cliff-like north shore of Willoughby Bay.

Climate

The main reason why there are no forests or rivers in Antigua is because the island does not get enough rainfall. It lies directly in the path of the North-East Trade Winds, and the wind blows from the east for ninety per cent of the time. With little high ground and no forests to attract rainfall the annual average figure for the whole island is about 45 inches. As the ground in the central plain is unsuitable for deep penetration of water an enormous proportion of rainwater runs into the sea. Most of what passes into the subsoil is collected in the hilly south-western region. Throughout its history the island has suffered from prolonged droughts and a general shortage of fresh water. The problem has been tackled in a variety of ways. In the past wells were sunk in areas where ground water collected, and numerous small ponds were created for the use of animals and subsistence farmers. Since the first buildings were erected it has been the practice to collect rain-water from the roofs in tanks or cisterns, and still today this provides the main supply of fresh water in the majority of Antiguan houses. In the late 1960s a large, shallow reservoir was constructed in the centre of the island to provide the main source of a piped fresh water supply. Today, with an increasing population and an expanding tourist industry, the total supply of fresh water can barely meet the demand. The situation became critical during the 1980s and at one time water had to be imported. The construction of a desalination plant on the north coast at the end of the decade did much to alleviate the problem.

The low rainfall and more or less constant easterly breeze give Antigua one of the finest climates in the world. There are no wet and dry seasons as such. Based on records compiled during the past 130 years or more the most that can be said is that – in an average year – September, October and November are *likely* to be the rainiest months, and February, March and April the driest. The warmest time of the year is between August and October, when the temperature range is 80–89 °F (28–32 °C). The coolest months are December, January and February, with a temperature range of about 70–80 °F (21–28 °C). These idyllic conditions are interrupted from time to time by the passage of a tropical storm or hurricane – to which the whole of the Caribbean region is prone in certain months.

The 'hurricane season' lasts from the middle of July until the middle of October, with August the month in which they are most likely to occur. Antigua experienced two in August 1950 but then none directly until hurricane 'Luis' struck the island at the beginning of September 1995. Because of the excellent early warning system no lives were lost; although considerable damage was sustained to property, forcing several of the major hotels to close down, the airport re-opened within thirty-six hours and life rapidly returned to normal for most people. By the middle of the following year it would have been difficult for a visitor to the island to have known that anything untoward had taken place.

Earthquakes

It would be inappropriate not to mention that Antigua, besides being threatened by the possibility of a hurricane each year, is also subject to occasional earth tremors and very frequent earthquakes. The majority of the tremors are so minor as to pass quite unnoticed. The most recent earthquake was in 1974 when a few public buildings, particularly in St John's, were damaged. The threat from such earth movements is by no means as great as in places like San Francisco or Tokyo, and with no densely populated areas or high-rise buildings the danger to life is minimal.

The coastline

No description of Antigua would be complete without mention of three features of the coastline – the beaches, the salt ponds and the reefs. Popular local opinion holds that the island has 365 beaches; one for each day of the year. While this may or may not be so (and there is certainly no documentary evidence of their existence), Antigua has an extremely long coastline for such a small island. This is over 90 miles in length and there are ample bays and coves containing stretches of fine white sand. These beaches form one of

Antigua's greatest natural attractions, and some of them rank amongst the finest in the entire Caribbean.

The salt ponds which are found behind many of the beaches, especially along the west coast, are another distinctive feature. They were probably created by shallow bays being cut off from the sea by the growth of mangroves and other plants. These caused sand to be deposited and to build up into bars, and allowed the enclosed water

Johnsons Point Beach (CHRIS HUXLEY)

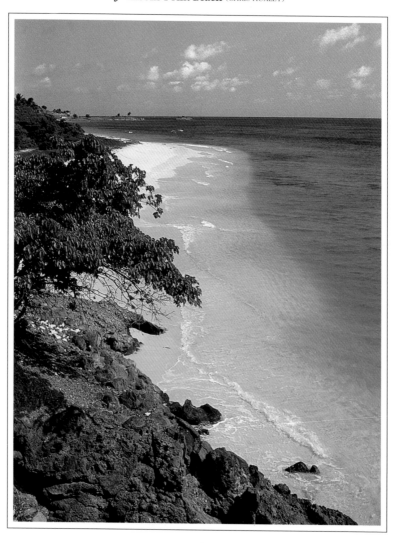

to become brackish. Eventually they turned into the swamps or shallow ponds that are seen today. The largest single area, called The Flashes, is at the head of Five Islands Harbour. While it is not easy to discern the natural beauty of large areas of mostly stagnant water and mangroves, the ponds are of considerable ecological significance. All are the habitat of various species of wildlife and some, containing evidence of the prehistoric settlement of the island, are of archaeological interest. The view of conservationists is that it would be unwise to tamper with any of them. This has been borne out in the past, when attempts to convert one or two into artificial boat harbours have failed, with unexpected and adverse results.

The extensive areas of coral reef, particularly on the northern and eastern sides of the island, are another prime national asset. A more or less continuous barrier reef about two miles offshore, containing areas with names such as Salt Fish Tail, Horseshoe Reef and Kettle Bottom Shoals, protects the whole of the north coast. From Long Island around the north-east coast as far as Green Island there are an enormous number of coral reefs and patches surrounding each islet, and extending across the mouth of each bay and inlet. In the south-east Willoughby Bay is cut off at its entrance by a much bigger Horseshoe Reef, through which there are narrow passages, while the whole of the shoreline between Falmouth Harbour and the south-western corner of the island is fringed by coral. About a mile offshore to the south of Johnsons Point in the south-west is Cades Reef – a huge area of reef about one and a half square miles in extent and within a few feet of the surface. While all of these reefs are of course highly dangerous to shipping they are a most important natural resource. Besides assisting in the creation of the island's splendid beaches, they also provide a breeding and feeding ground for many varieties of fish and shellfish. They also protect the windward coasts from erosion and provide calm water in the bays and inshore passages.

The beach at Half Moon Bay (overleaf) (MICHAEL BOURNE)

| 3 |
Natural history

Plants

On the first approach the coast appears rough and barren, but as the voyager draws nearer, hills and valleys open to his view, and the shore puts on an appearance of luxuriant vegetation.

While this description from the opening pages of *Antigua and the Antiguans* still holds true today, the appearance of the island from a distance is as deceptive now as it was in the 1840s. The forest with which the island was covered when it was sighted by Columbus in 1493 disappeared long before Mrs Lanaghan's day, and the luxuriant aspect is created by large areas of bush interspersed with farmland. The hilly region contains plenty of trees with mahogany, logwood, loblolly, tamarind, white cedar, cinnamon and turpentine growing together with coconut and other palms, mango and breadfruit, to give the closest approximation to a forest in Antigua. The rest of the island is very open, with large tracts of pasture, arable land and bush well intermingled, and with the occasional grove of trees or small coconut plantations. Most of the bush consists of various species of acacia, all of which are referred to locally as 'cassie'.

Standing here and there among the bush will be seen specimens of the tree-like agave, known as the Dagger Log, whose yellow blooms are the national flower. In days gone by the plant was used for a variety of purposes, including tinder, cord from its leaf fibre, and logs for making rafts. Growing to a height of over twenty feet, the plant flowers only once in its life of perhaps twenty years, after which it dies.

Around the coast, providing shade at the back of most beaches, are coconut, tamarind and casuarina, together with sea-grape and manchineel trees. The sea-grape is a low tree with large broad leaves which bears clusters of small velvety berries which, when ripe and purple in colour, are edible. The notorious manchineel on the other hand is to be avoided; the sap is caustic and poisonous as are the small apple-like fruit. Mangrove trees grow profusely around the heads of some of the bays and creeks, especially on the north-east coast between Parham Harbour and Mercers Creek Bay.

Pomegranate flower (CHRIS HUXLEY)

Pomegranate fruit (CHRIS HUXLEY)

Pineapples (CHRIS HUXLEY)

Water lily (CHRIS HUXLEY)

As if to offset the vast expanse of green vegetation, whether wild or cultivated, which covers most of the island, Antiguans grow a profusion of flowering trees and shrubs. At any time of the year many varieties of hibiscus, oleander and bougainvillaea, usually grown as hedges, will be seen in the garden of even the smallest house. The flamboyant or poinciana tree, which bears a bright red flower, is also very common.

In the same small garden with its hibiscus or oleander hedge almost always there will be at least one kind of fruit tree. Although little fruit, other than pineapples, is grown on a proper commercial basis, there are few householders who do not have a lime, breadfruit, mango, paw-paw, guava or some other fruit tree 'in the yard'. Some fruit are picked all the year round while others have their seasons, but there is always a big selection available. The surplus from the larger private orchards and the produce of small market gardens inevitably finds a retail outlet, and all the fruit mentioned above and many more can be found on sale around the island.

The innate conservatism of the standard hotel menu prevents many varieties of local fruit from appearing on it. The visitor who accepts this and foregoes the opportunity of sampling a grafted mango, a paw-paw or a sugar apple, bought from a street huckster, will miss a rare treat. The visitor who finds such things on the menu will know that he is staying in a superior hotel. (Having said this, a word of advice concerning one of these fruit may be necessary. The proper way to eat a mango is to attack it with one's teeth, ignoring any attempt at delicacy with knife, fork or spoon. A ripe, grafted juli mango eaten while standing or sitting in the sea is unbelievably good – the salt water adding to the flavour and washing away all traces of the flesh and juice which, if the mango is to be enjoyed to the full, must gather on the eater's face ...)

Animals

The wild animal life of Antigua is very limited. Indeed, as Mrs Lanaghan pointed out, 'In an island like Antigua, destitute of every wild animal of larger growth than a rabbit or a rat, it may be deemed risible to talk about its zoology ...'. Today it is highly unlikely that there are any rabbits remaining on the island as the 'rat' to which she referred was probably the mongoose, which had been introduced during the 18th century. This animal was brought to the West Indies to keep down the rats and snakes in the sugar cane fields. In Antigua it soon rid the island of all its snakes, but when it began to attack poultry and the wild bird life it was realised that its introduction was not an unqualified blessing. Throughout the West Indies the mongoose is now classified as a pest: in Antigua it is probably the only wild animal that most visitors will ever see.

Although there are precious few snakes left (see page 92) there are numerous lizards. The common tree lizard will be seen on almost any tree or fence. Normally green, it has the power of changing its colour like a chameleon. It feeds on insects and small buds and is perfectly harmless. The ground lizard, which is much larger and darker, will sometimes be seen, or more likely heard, scuttling about among fallen leaves and vegetation. It too is harmless and will run away if approached. Anyone who sights an even bigger member of the lizard family, the iguana, will be very fortunate. These are found only in the drier eastern part of the island, well away from all human habitation, and sightings in recent years have been very rare.

Birds

The bird life of Antigua is considerably more interesting than the animal life, but is still not prolific. The bird population appears to fluctuate from year to year, being very sensitive to the amount of rainfall and the effect that this has on the number of insects available for food. Over 140 species have been observed, of which about 90 are seen regularly. The ornithologist will find much of interest at any time of the year as many of the species are migratory and the bird population varies from season to season. Some of the more common resident birds are so much in evidence that they cannot fail to be noticed by even the most casual observer.

Just as the banana is probably the most common fruit in Antigua, a small, yellow-breasted bird called the Bananaquit is one of the commonest birds. This can be seen any day together with another bird of much the same size, the Lesser Antillean Bullfinch, which is black or grey with a reddish breast. These are seen around most hotels with outdoor dining areas, and they are fond of taking sugar and crumbs from the tables. One or two species of humming bird are native to the island, and these will be seen and heard around any flowering shrub. The commonest is probably the Antillean Crested Hummingbird, which is very small and dark with a bright green crest. In the

21

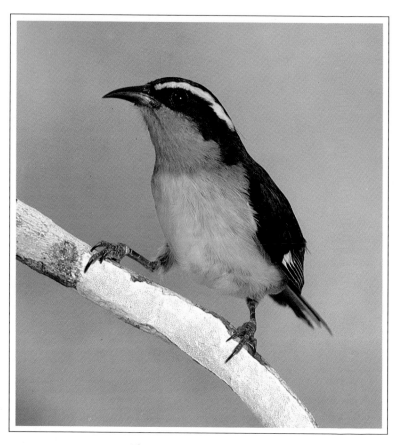

The Bananaquit (R.P. FFRENCH)

countryside the most conspicuous bird is the Cattle Egret, a small white heron with a bright yellow bill. It is seen in the company of grazing animals, often standing on the back of a cow, or where ploughing is taking place. In the evenings large roosts of these birds are found in the trees around various ponds.

Anywhere around the coast the Brown Pelicans are unmistakable. This large water bird, native to the Americas, is the only pelican indigenous to the islands of the Caribbean. They are usually sighted in small groups either sitting on rocks or flying low over the sea. They are spectacular birds in flight and make a lot of noise when diving into the water after fish. That this bird is very common can be discovered from a quick glance at a map of Antigua, on which are shown

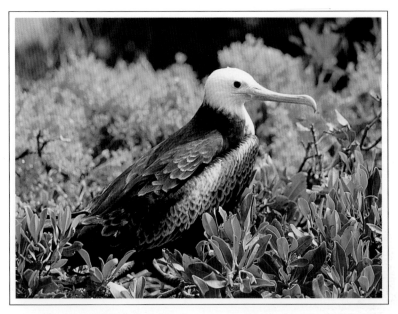

The Frigate Bird is found in the swamps of Barbuda (CHRIS HUXLEY)

no less than three Pelican Islands and a group of Pelican Rocks. Many other varieties of shore birds and waders frequent the salt ponds and reservoirs. Several species of gulls and terns live on some of the small islets off the north-east coast, where Great Bird Island, Little Bird Island, Bird Island and Bird Islet presumably all take their names from the birds' habitats.

Marine life

The waters around Antigua abound with marine life, but contain little that need bother the swimmer, snorkeler or skin-diver. As in any tropical waters there are potentially troublesome things such as sharks, barracuda, spiney sea urchins and, at certain times of the year, large jellyfish. There have been very few reports of sharks coming close inshore within living memory, and the observation of elementary precautions will ensure that none of the others need worry anyone in the sea. The diver or swimmer experienced enough to venture out to the more distant reefs will presumably know and observe the basic rules about not poking into crevices, bleeding in the water or making a lot of noise. The less adventurous will find the shallow water off a beach virtually devoid of marine life, but it is unwise to wade where the seabed is covered by seaweed (the most common type is called eelgrass) as this may hide sea urchins.

Apart from the great variety of coral formations and their attendant tropical fish to be seen by the snorkeler and diver, the sea around Antigua also supports many types of edible fish. The local fishermen are able to provide a reasonable supply of fish such as Grouper, Parrotfish, Snapper and Grunts, as well as lobsters, to meet the local demand. There are also fish such as Kingfish, Marlin, Wahoo and Tuna to interest the sport fishing enthusiast. Most species migrate annually through the eastern Caribbean chain of islands, and the best season for Antigua is from February to June.

| 4 |
A brief history

Pre-Columbus

There is evidence that the island we now know as Antigua has been inhabited, although not continuously, for about the past 4000 years. The earliest known inhabitants were the Ciboney ('Stone people'), who came to the island from the mainland of South America around 500 BC, and of whom not much is recorded except that they were nomadic and had no knowledge of agriculture. Some stone tools and evidence of their considerable consumption of shellfish have been discovered at one or two places around the coast. The first people to leave behind any major evidence of their occupation of the island were the Arawaks. These probably reached Antigua about two thousand years ago. They originated in South America, in the area between the Orinoco and Amazon rivers, and gradually spread through the island chain of the eastern Caribbean. They practised agriculture and developed a settled village life. Lots of tools, pottery fragments and decorated shells have been unearthed at several sites, again on or near the coast.

The Arawak occupation probably ended in about 1200 AD when they moved on to other islands further west, or were overrun by the Caribs. These people, who of course have given their name to the Caribbean Sea, also originated in South America and spread northwards through the islands. They were much more war-like and less pastoral than the Arawaks. No trace has yet been found of their settlement of the island, but they continued to visit it – often with bloody results – until the end of the 17th century. Based on rather slender evidence (an unverified entry in a Carib-French dictionary of the mid-17th century) it is thought that the Carib name for the island was something like 'Waladli' – a disagreeably unmelodious appellation very much in keeping with the nature of their society. Their name for Barbuda, from the same source, was even more unpleasant. The reader has only to ask herself if she would like a vacation in, or enjoy being a citizen of, the 'State of Waladli and Wa'omoni' to appreciate the debt owed by at least two West Indian islands to the first European discoverer.

Discovery and settlement

In November 1493, on his second voyage to the New World, Columbus sighted the island and gave it the name *Santa Maria la Antigua* (after a famous statue of The Virgin in Seville Cathedral). In doing so he not only started its recorded history but provided it with a name of considerable grace and harmony, even though it was soon shortened to just Antigua. And here perhaps is the place to stress that the name is pronounced as 'Anteega' and not as if it rhymed with 'how big you are'. Columbus did not land and very little happened in the island for the next 130 years. The Spanish, English and French made desultory efforts at settlement, but failed through the lack of fresh water and raids by the Caribs. The first permanent European settlement was founded in 1632, when a group of English colonists arrived from the nearby island of St Kitts which had been settled some eight years earlier. The first settlement was in the south in the area now called Old Road. Except for a few months during 1666 and 1667, when the French occupied it, Antigua remained in British hands thereafter.

Plantations and slavery

To begin with the island was used for growing tobacco (another word from the Carib language), but by the end of the 17th century this had been replaced totally by sugar cane. The production of sugar was far more profitable and it remained the basis of the economy until well into the second half of the 20th century. For the first thirty years or so after the initial settlement the population was very small. It began to rise quickly only when the conversion from tobacco to sugar production started. The planters found that indentured white servants and labourers gave poor results, and so turned to the importation of slaves from Africa to work their plantations. In 1680 the population was about 4500, made up of almost equal numbers of whites and blacks. Thirty years later the white population had increased only fractionally while the black proportion had swelled to nearly 13 000. As Antigua progressed through the 18th century the planters became firmly established as men of wealth and substance. With an economy based entirely on sugar being produced by an army of slaves, the island was divided up into numerous estates (a map of the early 19th century lists 161 by name). Each estate was centred on an 'estate house' and had at least one windmill to grind the cane and extract the juice.

The estate system has had an ineradicable effect on the island. Most of the estate names remain in use, serving as district names outside the villages and within the six parishes into which, outside St John's, Antigua is divided. The windmills, now of course all abandoned and sail-less, can be seen everywhere. They are an enduring and in some ways most befitting memorial to the succeeding generations of slaves who operated them. This was recognized in 1994

Ffryes Mill (PADDY BROWNE)

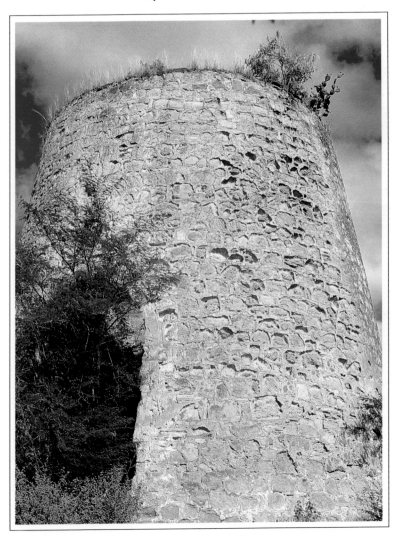

when the sugar mill tower, of which there are well over a hundred scattered throughout the island, was declared to be the official historic symbol.

The estate houses, which a writer in the early 1800s described as being '... embosomed in trees having more of the appearance of country mansions in England than almost any others in the West Indies' have largely disappeared or fallen into disrepair. Those which are still inhabited or have been converted to some other use excite very little interest. The stone towers of the windmills on the other hand remain conspicuous and intriguing in every part of the island: impervious to weather, hurricanes and earthquakes they are seemingly indestructible and as such make a very suitable national symbol.

Emancipation and the decline of sugar

Sugar production continued to be extremely profitable until towards the end of the 18th century. After that, as Great Britain found other cheaper sources of sugar, the economy of Antigua began to decline. This decline matched the increase in the demands for an end to slavery. The slave trade was made illegal by Great Britain in 1807, and this was followed in 1834 by the abolition of slavery itself. In Antigua at that time there were just over 29 000 slaves, about 4000 'Free Coloureds' and barely 2000 whites.

The slaves were made completely free on 1 August 1834, but within a few weeks of their emancipation the majority had returned to the estates to work as free labourers. They had little choice as there were very few areas of free land available for them to settle on and cultivate. Those that refused to continue living on an estate began to settle in 'independent villages' with names like Freetown, Liberta and Freemans Village. Others went to live in villages which grew up around Non-conformist churches which had ministered to them while they were still slaves – places like Newfield, Bethesda and All Saints. By 1842 nearly thirty villages had been established and the map of Antigua began to take on the aspect it bears today.

As the freed slaves and their descendants started along the road to full political independence, the economy continued to wane. This was brought about by the fall in the value of West Indian sugar and by the unwillingness of the planters to turn to other crops. As a result many estates were either abandoned or incorporated into others as the 19th century progressed. By the beginning of the 20th century ownership of the estates was in the hands of comparatively few proprietors. By the mid-1940s most of the arable land belonged to one company. The effect this had on the ordinary Antiguan, the quality of his life and his standard of living, was devastating. A field worker's daily rate of pay in 1845 was one shilling; one hundred years later it varied between one and one and a half shillings if he worked on a large estate, and was *less* than one shilling if he had the misfortune to be employed on a small estate. Throughout this period Antigua remained a British colony, with a Governor exercising power through his Executive and Legislative Councils. Half of the members only of the latter were elected, with the electorate confined to whites and those blacks who could meet certain property and income qualifications.

The rise of Trade Unionism and the Second World War

The first major event to upset this depressing and stagnant state of affairs took place in 1939 with the passing of the Trade Union Act. This permitted the workers to act together to press for higher wages, better conditions and shorter hours. The first Trade Union in Antigua was registered the following year. Although this had an immediate effect on the life of the island a much greater event – the outbreak of the Second World War – must be considered as even more important to the creation of the Antigua we see today.

In an agreement with Great Britain reached in 1941 the USA leased sites for military bases in Antigua and other West Indian islands. In Antigua the arrival of large numbers of American servicemen and civilian contractors, and the need to erect their base facilities in a hurry, had an immediate and lasting effect on the way of life. To begin with local labour was hired at wage rates much higher than those paid by local employers. The 1941 sugar crop suffered from a shortage of field labourers, and many men refused to return to that kind of work from then on. As the war progressed the bases also provided some technical training. Labourers who remained working on them had the opportunity to become skilled or semi-skilled technicians – something most would have considered inconceivable in 1939.

While it would not be true to say that the presence of so many Americans in the island (the population of which at the time was about 40 000) did not have its unpleasant aspects, the overall effect was to the benefit of the Antiguan people. The island gained

Fort James (CHRIS HUXLEY)

materially from the construction of roads, deep water piers, and most of all a proper air field. The bases themselves were run down quickly after the war ended, but by then it must have been obvious that the Caribbean region would remain very much within the sphere of influence of the USA. By 1945 many ordinary Antiguans had been given a glimpse of another way of life and the opportunities it had to offer. There remained the problems of bringing these opportunities within their grasp, and of ending the dependence of the island's economy on sugar. It was to solving these problems that the Antigua Trades and Labour Union started to devote its energies as soon as the war was over. By that time the Union had a new President, elected in 1943. In Vere Cornwall Bird the Antiguan people were to find a man with the energy, intelligence and political ability to deal with the problems, and to lead them along the final stretch of the hard and sometimes very bumpy road to independent nationhood.

VC Bird and independence

In 1945 Bird was elected to the Legislative Council, and he began his connection with the government of Antigua which continued for over forty years. Mostly through his efforts and those of a few of his colleagues in the Antigua Labour Party full adult suffrage was granted in 1951, followed five years later by the introduction of a Ministerial system of Government. The Executive Council with its nominated members remained, but now contained three full-time Ministers, of whom Bird was one. In 1961 further constitutional changes were introduced. The number of elected members to the Legislative Council was increased and Bird became the Chief Minister with responsibility for choosing his own Ministers from among the Council members. In 1965, having demonstrated that black Antiguans were quite capable of running their own country, Bird and his Government began negotiations with the British Government about ending colonial rule. These led to Antigua being granted independence 'in association with Great Britain' in February 1967. Under this new relationship Antigua had full control over its internal affairs, but left the responsibility for defence and external affairs in British hands. Bird of course became the island's first Premier.

Throughout the years leading up to 'Associated Statehood' the role of sugar as the dominant factor in the economy had declined steadily. By 1965 Antigua Syndicate Estates, the company which by then owned all the sugar estates and the single sugar factory, was in great financial trouble. Two years later, in order to protect the jobs of several thousand workers and to secure the land for the people of Antigua, the assets of the company were bought by the Government. It was somehow very befitting that the last vestiges of the 'Plantocracy' should have disappeared in the same year that Antigua achieved Statehood. Bird was out of office between 1971 and 1976, and it was during this period that the sugar crop was abandoned and the factory closed down. In 1972, some 300 years after the crop was introduced, the reign of 'King Sugar' in Antigua came to an end.

The island remained an Associated State until 1 November 1981, when it became the major part of the totally independent country of Antigua and Barbuda. By then Bird had dominated the political scene for so long that all Antiguans, regardless of their colour, background or political affiliations, must have felt it only right and proper that he should become the State's first Prime Minister. It is worth repeating that the majority of the important events in Antiguan history – as far as Antiguans are concerned – have taken place since 1939, well within the lifetime of a still considerable proportion of the present population. During this period British governors and administrators came and went, few leaving any lasting impression on the island, while Bird remained there throughout – his name becoming increasingly synonymous with Antigua – until he retired from office in 1994, to be succeeded as Prime Minister by one of his sons.

| 5 |
The economy

Agriculture

Until after the Second World War the economy of Antigua depended almost entirely on the production of sugar cane. Sugar, molasses and rum accounted for well over ninety per cent of the island's exports up until 1945. After the war the agricultural scene began to change. The independent small farmers were encouraged to grow Sea Island Cotton, for which parts of the island are very well suited, and crops such as arrowroot and castor. The limiting factor to any agricultural diversification, though, was the unpredictable rainfall and the absence of streams or ponds for irrigation. A great deal to improve the situation had been carried out by the mid-1960s with the construction of earth-filled dams to form small reservoirs and ponds. By then sugar had become a marginal crop (disappearing altogether in 1972) and agricultural activity was concentrated on the growing of cotton, fruit and vegetables, and in the rearing of livestock.

The agricultural scene remains much the same today. Fruit and vegetables are grown almost exclusively for local consumption, although a good overseas market exists for the famous Antigua 'Black' pineapple. Cattle, sheep, goats and pigs are also reared for a purely local market. It will be obvious to even the most casual visitor that much of the island is uncultivated, and that large areas of what could be useful agricultural land are covered in bush and scrub. Probably less than five per cent of the total work-force is engaged in agriculture.

From being the basis of the island's economy for well over three hundred years, agriculture has become the least important factor in the space of perhaps one generation. Considering the long history of the estate system it is easy to understand why working on the land should be despised and rejected by so many Antiguans, but it is no less unfortunate that this should be the attitude. If the overall development of the State is to continue it will be important to utilise the land – one of its chief assets – to the full. The present official programme of encouraging the introduction of new crops and farming methods, while stimulating agricultural research and the involvement

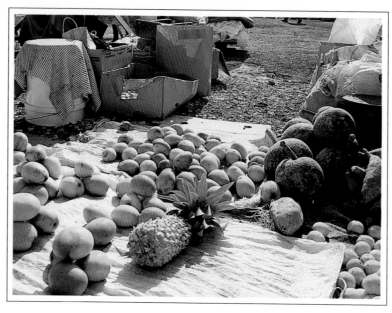

Market, St John's (CHRIS HUXLEY)

of foreign investors, is slowly changing the prevailing attitude. It is inconceivable that large numbers of Antiguans will ever be attracted back to the land, but there is no reason why, in time and with the proper assistance, the island's agricultural potential should not be realised.

Industry

Before about 1970 anyone talking about a factory in Antigua could only have been referring to the *sugar* factory. The manufacturing industry at the time comprised a rum distillery, a cotton ginnery, an edible oil plant, a few small furniture workshops, the odd pottery and one or two boat yards producing wooden boats. In 1965 the construction of a large (for the size of the island) oil refinery was begun on land to the north of St John's, which started operations two years later. The concept that this was something around which the industrial development of the island could be built was quickly destroyed by the oil fuel crisis of 1973–74. The refinery was forced to close down less than ten years after it opened. An attempt to reactivate it in the early 1980s proved abortive and it is now defunct.

Although the need for an industrial sector in the economy was recognised much earlier, the right conditions for its growth did not come into being until about 1970. By that time deep water port facilities had been constructed on the north side of St John's Harbour, and the airport had been improved and modernised in order to operate all types and sizes of aircraft. Despite the set-back caused by the closure of the oil refinery, the industrialisation of Antigua, in as far as this term can be applied to the island, continued throughout the next decade. The incentives being offered for the setting up of 'pioneer' industries were improved considerably in 1975 by the Fiscal Incentives Act. This made provision for tax holidays, import duty exemptions and the unrestricted repatriation of profits for foreign investors. These incentives, together with the building of a 'factory estate' close to the airport and the presence of a large and willing work-force (with a high rate of unemployment), have had the desired results. Industry, which is fairly evenly divided between local and overseas ownership, is concerned mainly with light manufacturing or assembling enterprises. The goods produced are mostly for the local and regional markets, with the remainder being for export to North America.

At the same time the number of cottage industries has also increased. Small workshops still make hand-crafted furniture, the traditional wooden boats and ceramic ware. They have now been joined by others, often located in the most unexpected places, producing such things as floor tiles, batteries and concrete garden furniture. The independent spirit of the Antiguan continues to flourish, perhaps in reaction to the advent of the factory and assembly line, but possibly also to the more servile aspects of tourism.

Tourism

The arrival of the US forces in 1941 may have given a few of the more astute Antiguans a foretaste of what lay ahead once the war was over, but it is unlikely that anyone could have foreseen how tourism would come to dominate the economy within the next quarter of a century. In 1950 there was one beach hotel, by 1960 there were seven, and by 1970 the total was nineteen. With the

Jumby Bay Resort, Long Island (overleaf) (CHRIS HUXLEY)

opening of the deep water harbour in 1968 the island started to attract far more cruise ships, and within three years four or five ships were handled each week during the 'tourist season'. After the improvements to the airport, carried out in 1970, Antigua was in a position to attract tourists of every sort, not only from North America but from Europe as well. The next decade saw a boom in the construction of all kinds of holiday accommodation.

The tourist industry is now the mainstay of the country's economy and its principal foreign exchange earner. At least 250 000 visitors arrive by air each year, with about 300 000 paying shorter visits in the cruise ships. Accommodation of every kind is now available for tourists, provided by hotels, resorts, guest-houses, and in a wide range of villas and apartments. About one sixth of the total workforce is employed directly or indirectly in the industry. The concept of previous years, in which the bulk of visitors came in the fairly short 'season' from mid-December to mid-April, no longer applies. While the numbers fall during the summer months there is plenty of tourist activity throughout the year. Although some of the hotels still close during what used to be called the 'off-season', the visitor is assured of the same service and facilities from the industry as a whole, regardless of the time of year.

The hidden factor

There is one other aspect of the economy, but one about which very little information is available. This is the contribution made by Antiguans living abroad in the form of cash remittances made to their relatives in the island. It is impossible to measure the overall effect this has on the economy as a whole: at the same time, for anyone acquainted with a cross-section of society, it is impossible not to recognise the importance of this 'hidden factor' to the personal economies of many of the poorer Antiguans.

| 6 |
The people

Population

Antigua, like many of the other small West Indian islands, has a large proportion of its citizens living abroad permanently. Emigration has been a constant factor in the life of the island since at least the beginning of this century. The building of the Panama Canal between 1903 and 1914 attracted many men from Antigua and all the other British West Indian islands. Others emigrated to Cuba, the Dominican Republic, Canada and the USA. The development of oil refineries in the Dutch islands of Curaçao and Aruba in the late 1930s caused more Antiguans to leave, but the largest migration of all took place after the Second World War. This was brought about by the demand for labour in Great Britain, and only halted by the introduction of controls on immigration by the British Government in 1962. Since then Canada and the USA have received the majority of Antiguan emigrants, but limited by the enforcement of quotas and other restrictions.

It is now impossible even to guess at the number of Antiguans living overseas, but it should not be forgotten that they still make a significant contribution to the economy. Constant coming and going makes it difficult to assess the permanent population of the island, but it is probably no more than about 65 000. Most are of African descent, with perhaps ten per cent of mixed black and white ancestry. In none of the censuses taken between 1860 and 1960 were more than five per cent of non-African descent, and usually the figure was much smaller. Today Antigua has a much more cosmopolitan society with, in addition to citizens of British, Portuguese, Syrian, Lebanese, Chinese, Haitian and Dominican origin, a sizeable community of North Americans and Europeans who have retired to the island.

This is still only a superficial picture of Antiguan society. Before 1962 there were no restrictions on movement between any of the then British West Indian islands. Because of its focal position in the eastern Caribbean, Antigua probably saw more movement of people, both in and out, than many of the other islands. As a result many Antiguans were born in other places as far apart as Guyana and Jamaica, and many more have a parent or parents born outside the island. It would

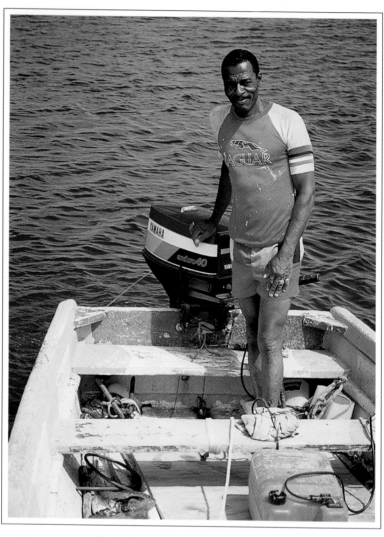

Guide for bird sanctuary, Barbuda (CHRIS HUXLEY)

be stretching the point to claim that Antiguan society is a Caribbean federation in microcosm but the diverse origins of the people, black and white, have helped to create the outward-looking and cosmopolitan attitude which is now assisting the country's development. The influence of Great Britain, North America and the rest of the Caribbean can be traced through many aspects of Antiguan life, but they are perhaps most apparent in the educational system and in religious matters.

Education

The State provides free primary and secondary education. There are a few private, fee-paying schools, in some cases affiliated to churches. All provide an education which is grounded very much in the British system and, until recently, orientated towards obtaining British educational certificates and qualifications. The emphasis has now moved towards the use of new curricula developed within the Caribbean region, and a type of education more suited to the social and economic development of the island. The Antigua State College, besides training teachers, also offers technical and vocational training to suit local requirements. Any higher education has to be obtained abroad. Almost invariably this will be at the University of the West Indies (with campuses in Jamaica, Trinidad and Barbados) or at one of the cheaper colleges in the US Virgin Islands, the USA or Canada.

Religion

It must be a matter for some regret that the attempts to create a nation and a sense of nationhood are now, to some extent, being undermined by an unusual degree of divisiveness in religious matters.

St Philips Church (CHRIS HUXLEY)

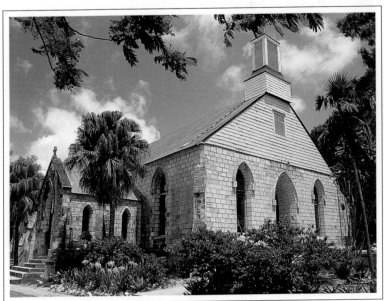

Even the most transient visitor cannot fail to notice the large number of churches in Antigua. The more innocent might assume that Antiguans are an unusually religious and God-fearing people. Unfortunately this is not quite true, and they are no more and no less devout than any others.

The Christian religion arrived in Antigua with the first settlers, and the Anglican Church remained the 'Established' Church until 1875. In its earlier days, as a local writer the Reverend Leslie Lett has stated, it was '... ecclesiastically and racially, entirely and unrepentantly narrow and intolerant ...'. This attitude changed after Emancipation, but long before then the Moravian and Methodist Churches had begun to minister to the slaves and to educate them. As a result the Anglican Church was very much identified with the 'plantocracy' while the mass of the slaves, later the black free labourers, belonged to the Nonconformist Churches. It was a long time before this division ended. Between 1835 and 1882 over 2000 Portuguese came to the island, mostly from Madeira, to work as labourers. While not all of them stayed their continuing presence brought about the establishment of the Roman Catholic Church in Antigua in 1859.

Thereafter, until the 1960s, the Anglican, Moravian, Methodist and Roman Catholic Churches ministered to at least 85 per cent of the population. Since then this proportion has fallen steadily, and in recent years dramatically, with the arrival of numerous fundamentalist Sects and Churches. On the one hand this trend away from the ecumenical leanings of the Churches which originated in Europe and are deeply rooted in the life and history of Antigua, towards the intolerance and occasional bigotry of Churches originating in the southern USA and quite unfamiliar with the West Indian life, is to be deplored. On the other hand it can also be viewed as another manifestation of the Antiguan spirit of independence. While each individual in Antigua has not yet built his own church it often seems, from the ever-increasing number of tabernacles, bethels, halls and temples all around the island, that this must be a common aspiration.

Sport

There is one aspect of life in Antigua which so far has felt little North American influence. The sports played remain very much as in the days when the island was under British rule, and cricket – that most English of games – must be considered the national sport. Indeed, since the inclusion during the 1970s of two Antiguan players in the combined West Indies team which plays at an international level, it has become almost impossible to write about Antigua without mentioning the game. Before Vivian Richards and Anderson Roberts were selected, players from any of the smaller islands had been effectively debarred from playing for the West Indies; since their selection Antigua has never been quite the same. Both men became folk-heroes, featured in calypsoes and on postage stamps, and had streets in St John's named after them. They have since been followed into the Test team by a number of other players, and the Antiguan contribution to present-day international cricket now easily rivals that of Barbados or Jamaica.

The only other game worth mentioning here is one which should properly be relegated to the status of an indoor table game. Most visitors however will probably see *Warri* – a type of board game for two players – being played outdoors with a degree of noise and movement more suited to more physical and energetic pastimes. The game originates from Africa, as one of the 'hole and pebble' games which started in Egypt over 5000 years ago. The word 'warri' is an African word for houses, and the game is played on a wooden board with two rows of hollows called 'houses', in and out of which each player moves some of his two dozen pebbles ('seeds'). It can be played at a fairly casual level or more seriously using a strategy which matches chess in its range. The game is played in other Caribbean islands but appears to have a much greater following in Antigua, and is now very much identified with the island. Because more has been written about cricket than any other game it is impossible to suggest any one book which would explain the game to the uninitiated. But as far as I or the author know there is only one book devoted to explaining the game of *Warri*. This is *How to play Warri* written by an American, David Chamberlin, but published and printed in Antigua. This deals with both the simple and advanced mechanics of play, and is readily available from shops in St John's.

Cricket Test between the West Indies and England at the Recreation Ground, St John's (overleaf) (PATRICK EAGAR)

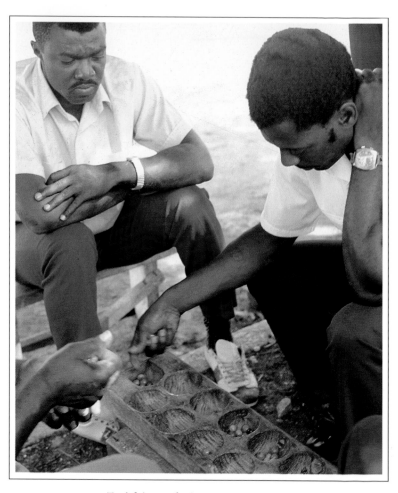

Taxi drivers playing *Warri* (ANNE BOLT)

Government

After independence Antigua and Barbuda remained a monarchy with Queen Elizabeth II as the Head of State. Her representative in the State is the Governor-General. Parliament consists of the House of Representatives and the Senate. Representatives are elected by popular vote from sixteen constituencies in Antigua and one in Barbuda, and a general election must be called at least every five years. Senators are appointed by the Governor-General on the advice of the Prime Minister and the Leader of the Opposition. The Prime

Codrington Post Office and Treasury, Barbuda (CHRIS HUXLEY)

Minister heads a Cabinet of Ministers who administer the State. All legislation is introduced in the House of Representatives and then passed to the Senate for review and assent. The whole form of Government is modelled very much on the British Parliamentary System.

While pomp and pageantry play their part in Antigua as much as in Great Britain or elsewhere, there is a degree of informality among the dignitaries and leaders of the State which is very much in keeping with the West Indian way of life. It is not unusual to see the Governor-General at the wheel of his own car, nor to queue with his wife in a local supermarket. Cabinet Ministers and Senators are not the lofty and guarded figures found in some other countries. Ministerial office does not prevent its holder from being stopped for a chat in the street, and most Senators can be found, when the Senate is not sitting, carrying on with perfectly ordinary jobs in St John's.

One important feature of any ceremonial display is of course the national flag. This was flown for the first time when Antigua became an 'Associated State' in 1967. Its various components were described by the local artist who designed it:

The red, blue and black to symbolize the dynamism, hope and the African heritage of the Antiguan people; the golden sun to symbolize the dawn of an new era; the gold, blue and white to represent the island's natural attractions of sun, sea and sand; and the 'V' sign to depict victory.

Whether this amount of symbolism should be read into the flag of one tiny nation is open to question, but it certainly cannot be mistaken for the flag of any other country. The design is bold and distinctive, and contrasts beautifully with the normal background of green hills and blue sky. It is flown with pride from public buildings and appears in various representations in most of the tourist literature and on souvenirs of all kinds.

In addition to symbols like the flag, the sugar mill tower and the dagger log which have already been mentioned, and the dish and fruit which are covered later in this book, there is also a national dress. Introduced only in 1994, and based on the clothing worn by women on special occasions in the immediate post-emancipation era, the ensemble consists of a white apron worn over a colourful madras dress with a matching madras head-wrap tied in a distinctive way. There is also a male version, consisting of a madras waistcoat worn with a white shirt, black pants, and a straw hat with a madras band. It is to be seen (if it is to be seen at all, having not met with universal approbation) in St John's on infrequent occasions connected with some national celebration.

The courts and the law

As is to be expected in a Parliamentary democracy, the judiciary is totally independent of the Administration and exercises its authority in accordance with the Constitution and the Laws of Antigua. The regional, as opposed to the purely national, thread can be traced to the High Court judges, who are shared with five other States. Any appointment or dismissal requires the approval of all six States. High Court sentences are subject to review by the Eastern Caribbean Court of Appeal, which sits in Antigua from time to time. Final appeal to the Privy Council in England is still available in some cases. The less serious offences are dealt with in Magistrates' Courts.

Law and order are maintained by the Royal Antigua Police Force, made up of uniformed men and women who do not, in the normal course of events, carry firearms. Once again the regional influence is felt as many members come from other islands, and add to the impartiality of policing a small community. The Police Force is also responsible for the seaward defence of the State, manning a patrol boat used for anti-smuggling duties, fishery protection and search and rescue operations as required.

Antigua and the outside world

It is in Antigua's membership of various international and regional organisations that the State acknowledges the three main influences on its life and history. Although it is a member of the British Commonwealth, owing allegiance to a European Queen, Antigua also recognises that it is an integral part of the Caribbean region as well as being very much part of the Americas. Membership of the Organisation of American States was obtained shortly after independence in 1981. Before that Antigua had played an important part in the creation of the Caribbean Community and Common Market (CARICOM), which exists to promote free trade among its members and to protect the growth of local industries. An equally important part was played in establishing the Organisation of Eastern Caribbean States (OECS), in order to extend economic co-operation and to harmonise foreign policy among the seven ex-British Windward and Leeward Islands.

With her membership of both the British Commonwealth and the Organisation of American States, Antigua could be said to have a foot in both camps, and to be maintaining links with both the past and the future. With its geographical advantages and present state of development the island is certainly well placed to play a significant role in the future – as the heart of the Caribbean.

Part 2

Foreground

| 7 |
Arriving in the island

The importance of Antigua's fine natural harbours, and its key position with regard to the main trade routes by sea to and from North America and Europe, were recognised from the earliest days of its settlement. In more recent times the combination of geographical location and a terrain suitable for the construction of an international airport has added to the island's importance. Antigua is now the focal point of a complicated network of air communications in the eastern Caribbean. There are daily flights to nearly all the other islands in the eastern Caribbean, as well as to New York ($3\frac{1}{2}$ hours) and Miami ($2\frac{1}{2}$ hours), with several flights each week to London (8 hours) and Toronto ($4\frac{1}{2}$ hours). The island is four hours behind Greenwich Mean Time and one hour ahead of Eastern Standard Time. There are five ports of entry into Antigua. St John's Deep Water Harbour caters for cruise ships and commercial shipping, and three much smaller ports are used by the numerous yachts which visit the island. The one which will be used by the majority of visitors, and certainly by nearly all those intending to stay for more than one day, is the airport.

VC Bird International Airport
The airport is situated on the north-eastern side of the island about four miles from St John's. It has a single 9000 foot runway capable of operating all types of aircraft, including wide-bodied 'jumbo' jets and Concorde. Over half of the 50 000 or more aircraft movements each year are scheduled flights. The island is served by at least half a dozen international airlines, along with several regional carriers. LIAT, the locally-owned airline, provides a daily service to all the islands between Puerto Rico and Trinidad, with routes to Venezuela, Guyana and the Dominican Republic. One or two small charter companies are also based at the airport.

Accommodation
The visitor intending to stay for more than one day is required to give an address before leaving the airport, and the necessary arrange-

52

ments should be made before arrival in order to prevent undue delay at the immigration officer's desk. To assist in planning a vacation or business trip the Antigua Tourist Board maintains offices in Canada, France, Germany, Great Britain, Italy and the USA:

Antigua Nevis Street
PO Box 363
St John's
Tel: 268-462-0480
Fax: 268-462-2483

Canada 60 St Clair Avenue East
Suite 304
Toronto
Ontario M4T 1N5
Tel: 416-961-3085
Fax: 416-961-7218

France 43 Avenue de Friedland
75008 Paris
Tel: 33-1-5375-1571
Fax: 33-1-5375-1569

Germany D-Thomasstrabe 11
61348 Bad Homburg
Tel: 49-6172-21504
Fax: 49-6172-21513

Great Britain 15 Thayer Street
London W1M 5LD
Tel: 171-486-7073
Fax: 171-486-9970

Italy Via Maria Alla Porta 9
20123 Milan
Tel: 39-2-877983
Fax: 39-2-877983

USA 610 Fifth Avenue
Suite 311
New York
NY 10020
Tel: 212-541-4117
Fax: 212-757-1607

25 S.E. 2nd Avenue
Suite 300
Miami
FL 33131
Tel: 305-381-6762
Fax: 305-381-7908

The island offers a complete range of accommodation, from first class luxury hotels and private clubs, through many medium and low-priced hotels and guest-houses, to self-catering cottages, villas and apartments. There is suitable accommodation for every requirement and every pocket. In addition to the travel guidance and literature which can be obtained from the offices of the Antigua Tourist Board, the prospective visitor can obtain more detailed information on the individual hotels which belong to the Association from:

Antigua Hotel and Tourist Association
Redcliffe Street, PO Box 454
St John's
Antigua
Tel: 268-462-0374
Fax: 268-462-3702

Unloading produce for the quayside market, St John's (MICHAEL BOURNE)

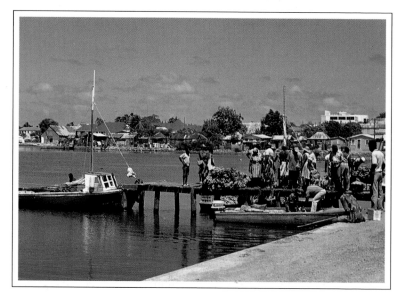

The rates quoted by the majority of hotels are based on the cost of accommodation without meals – European Plan (EP), or with breakfast and either lunch or dinner – Modified American Plan (MAP). The rates are subject to a ten per cent service charge, and also an eight and a half per cent Government tax. The revenue collected from the latter is used to develop the island's tourist facilities.

Immigration and customs

Entry into Antigua is kept as simple as possible. Citizens of the USA and Canada need only produce some form of identification. A passport only is required by citizens of Great Britain, the British Commonwealth countries, Japan, the EEC countries and the CARICOM countries. Anyone else will need both a passport and a visa. A return or onward ticket is required by every non-national entering the country by air. All visitors arriving by air will be given an immigration form to fill in before arrival. The carbon copy of this will be stamped by the immigration officer, who will keep the original. The copy must be retained and surrendered at the airport on departure. A departure tax of US$13.00 (or EC$35.00) is levied on all visitors staying for more than twenty-four hours; except those from CARICOM countries for whom the rate is lower, US$9.00 (EC$25.00).

Each adult is allowed to bring in two hundred cigarettes or fifty cigars or half a pound of pipe tobacco, together with one quart of wine or spirits and six ounces of perfume. The importation of any narcotics or so-called 'recreational drugs' is prohibited. Each visitor has to make a verbal baggage declaration, but all luggage is subject to Customs inspection.

Currency

The units of currency used in Antigua are dollars (EC$) issued by the Eastern Caribbean Central Bank. The denominations are notes worth five, ten, 20, 50 and 100 dollars, and coins worth one, two, five, ten, 25 and 50 cents, and one dollar. The EC dollar is linked to the US dollar at EC$2.70 to US$1.00. US currency is accepted everywhere at the rate fixed by the Antigua Chamber of Commerce at EC$2.60 to US$1.00. Travellers' cheques are accepted by many hotels, restaurants and stores, as are the usual credit cards. British and Canadian currency notes, and those of some other countries, are freely changeable

The *Jolly Roger* off Antigua (MICHAEL BOURNE)

at banks at rates which are quoted daily. All foreign currency transactions attract a one per cent Government levy. The visitor, because of the widespread use of the US dollar, should pay particular attention to the prices quoted for goods and services and always verify which dollar – the US or EC – is being quoted.

Transport

There is no organised bus service, with numbered routes, scheduled departures and marked stopping places. Instead there are a few routes, connecting the outlying parts of the island with St John's, along which individual bus owner-operators ply for hire from about 5.30 a.m. until nightfall. For the visitor with no firm schedule and who is in no hurry, these offer an interesting way of visiting some of the villages and meeting some of the villagers. In general the buses are reasonably comfortable and clean, and provide a decidedly cheap way of travelling. The alternatives are taxis or rented cars.

Taxis are available at all times in St John's and at the airport. They are also available at the Deep Water Harbour and at the major hotels during the hours when they may be needed. The majority are owner-operated and the drivers belong to an association which has controlled rates for the more popular trips and tours. Care should be taken to agree a fare with the driver (making sure about the currency being quoted) before starting any journey.

There are a variety of car rental firms. Vehicles can be rented through a combined bureau at the airport or from their individual premises in and around St John's. A local driving licence is needed. This can be arranged by the car rental company on presentation of a valid licence from the visitor's home country and payment of a US$20.00 fee. It must be remembered that, despite the number of left-hand drive vehicles to be seen, Antigua follows the British practice of driving on the left-hand side of the road. There is a general upper speed limit of forty mph throughout the island, except in St John's and the villages where it is twenty mph. As will become apparent very quickly, some of the roads in Antigua leave much to be desired and these speed limits will not be found irksome. The visitor who wishes to see as much of the island as possible is strongly recommended to hire a vehicle with four wheel drive – of which there are many available. The majority of the minor roads and tracks are unmotorable in anything else.

In keeping both with the generally informal tenor of Antiguan life, and the stubborn streak of independence in the Antiguan character, a number of highly individual driving habits are to be found amongst local drivers. The visitor must not be surprised at, or lose his patience with, the driver of the car in front who stops to chat in the middle of the road, turns right without signalling, or who parks on the inside corner of a right-angled bend. What, in New York or London, would produce apoplexy and rage among other road users, in Antigua produces only friendly toots on the horn and waving of the hand. The visitor should be prepared to smile and conform to local habits.

Clothing

The sensible visitor will also conform to local habits when it comes to clothing. While there are no regulations, bye-laws or restrictions on what can or cannot be worn, the wearing of swimsuits, very short shorts or see-through clothing in public places is not appreciated. Summer sports and casual wear is quite acceptable everywhere, and increasingly by both day and night. Some hotels require men to wear a jacket and tie in the evening, or perhaps on one or two evenings each week, but dinner jackets and evening dresses are now things of the past. One tourist brochure states that in the hotels 'a chic tropical look is expected'. The visitor who takes this dictum, which is open to wide interpretation, to apply to the whole of her stay on the island will be the one who suffers no embarrassment and earns the most local approbation.

Many of the shops in St John's and in the hotels specialise in providing day and evening wear for both men and women, with clothing ranging from tee-shirts to exotic, hand-screened cotton dresses, blouses, skirts and shirts. The visitor from even the least tropic-like parts of the world should have little difficulty in acquiring a suitable wardrobe.

The internationally known reggae singer, Kumasi, in Antigua (ANNE BOLT)

58

Entertainment

Evening entertainment for the visitor outside the major beach hotels is somewhat limited. The larger hotels provide some kind of regular nightly show, featuring steel bands, limbo dancers, calypso singers, dance troupes or keyboard performers. The standard varies and as the entertainers tend to move from one hotel to another throughout the week there is little point in the visitor going to another hotel 'to catch a show', as he may be accustomed to doing in other parts of the world. One or two of the superior hotels occasionally feature outside artistes for limited seasons, but their appearances are not advertised widely.

A more varied selection of evening entertainment is provided by some of the restaurants, a few in St John's but mostly in other parts of the island. This can include anything from crab racing to sessions by very professional jazz musicians. St John's usually has several discothèques. The most popular advertises itself as a night club: the others come and go as tastes change. For those who enjoy gambling there is a casino in the centre of the St John's waterfront. Others are to be found at the Halcyon Cove Hotel, the St James's Club, and at the Royal Antiguan Hotel.

On the whole the level of evening entertainment is not high. The visitor who is not staying in one of the hotels providing its own entertainment may well find that she quickly falls into the widespread Antiguan habit of retiring shortly after the evening meal and waking at daybreak. There is more than enough entertainment and enjoyment to be found in the island during the daylight hours to make up for the lack of a sophisticated night-life. While possibly only the world-weary will affirm that one steel band sounds much like another, or that if they have seen one limbo dancer you have seen them all, both the seasoned traveller and the novice 'first-timer' alike will soon observe that Antigua by day is quite unique.

Investment and finance

Enough has been said about the island's economy for the reader to appreciate why the Government is anxious to improve and expand the industrial sector. In spite of the priority given to promoting tourism and diversifying agriculture, there is still a large unemployment

Sunset at Falmouth Harbour (overleaf) (CHRIS HUXLEY)

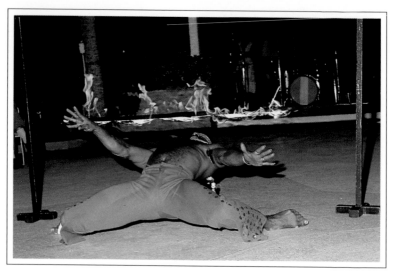

A limbo dancer performs the difficult trick of edging underneath a flaming bar (ANNE BOLT)

problem and an urgent need to train young Antiguans in new and more technical skills. Because of the difficulty in finding enough local capital to create more opportunities, legislation has been enacted which offers attractive incentives to foreign investors prepared to set up industrial enterprises. This policy has been reasonably successful and the number of new industrial concerns has increased steadily, but there is still the need for more. The island's work-force has an excellent record, free of disputes and the 'us against them' attitude found in many other parts of the world. With this background, the fiscal incentives, the ease of setting up a new factory, and Antigua's excellent communications, the island is an attractive investment area. Further information is available from:

Antigua Ministry of Economic Development
Queen Elizabeth Highway
St John's
Tel: 462-0092

At the end of 1982 Antigua and Barbuda was established as an Offshore Financial Centre, similar to the Bahamas or the Cayman Islands. This permits offshore corporations, banks and insurance companies to be set up with the minimum of Government interference, tax-free guarantees and exemption from foreign currency controls or levies. International Business Companies, which are now regularly incorporated in Antigua, can be set up for a down-payment of under US$2000 and cost less than half this much a year to maintain. Whether all such companies are strictly legitimate, or indeed whether offshore services of this nature in general are totally beneficial, is well outside the scope of this book. Plenty of information is available in the island for those interested in pursuing the subject of offshore finance further, some within walking distance of the airport terminal building.

Real estate

In addition to those wishing to invest in industry, private investors who would like to own a house or develop an area of land are also welcomed. Many North Americans and Europeans already own property in Antigua, and add to the cosmopolitan life of the island. Any visitor will be impressed by the amount of construction work which is taking place, and has been since the mid-1970s.

For anyone interested in buying property there is a complete range available, from 'time-share' apartments to luxurious villas. The real estate business is run on deceptively informal lines but its operatives are no less artful or any more principled here than anywhere else in the world. However, the reasonably astute outsider with the necessary capital, plenty of patience and sound legal advice should have little difficulty in buying a vacation or retirement home which is also a good investment.

Living and working in Antigua

The strong attraction for anyone wishing to live and work in Antigua, other than the superb climate, is that there is no personal income tax. For someone wishing to live on the island but not work this is immaterial, but before such a person can own land or property he must possess an 'alien's land-holding licence'. This is not that easy to obtain because of the long bureaucratic process through which any application goes. But, provided the proper qualifications are met and the correct procedure is followed – for which legal advice is essential – eventually it can be obtained.

A work permit is needed by anyone who is not a citizen who wants to work in Antigua. Provided there is no threat to the security of the State and that there is no Antiguan available to do the job for which it is requested, such a permit is readily granted. Anyone can apply for citizenship after establishing residency for seven years and meeting certain other criteria.

Public holidays

The following are observed as national holidays in Antigua and Barbuda:

New Year's Day
Good Friday
Easter Monday
Labour Day (first Monday in May)
Whit Monday
Caricom Day (first Monday in July)
Carnival Monday (first Monday in August)
Carnival Tuesday (first Tuesday in August)
Independence Day (1 November)
Christmas Day
Boxing Day (26 December)

Diplomatic representation

The following countries have diplomatic representation in Antigua:

Denmark
Hon Consul
PO Box 104
High Street
St John's
Tel: 462-0183

Germany
Hon Consul
PO Box 1259
St John's
Tel: 462-3174

Italy
Hon Consul
PO Box 1003
St John's
Tel: 460-1024

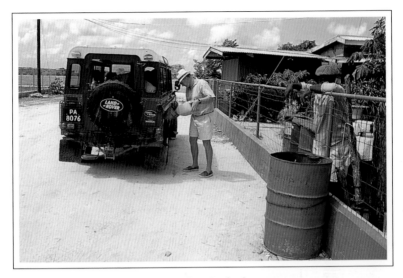

Codrington Gas Station, Barbuda (CHRIS HUXLEY)

Netherlands	Hon Consul PO Box 195 High Street St John's Tel: 462-0308
Norway	Hon Consul PO Box 194 High Street St John's Tel: 462-0858
United Kingdom	British High Commission Old Parham Road St John's Tel: 462-0008
Venezuela	Venezuelan Embassy Cross Street St John's Tel: 462-1574

| 8 |
The capital – St John's

The city of St John's sprawls all around the head of the large shallow bay which forms St John's Harbour. It has grown considerably since it was first laid out in the early 18th century, but particularly during the past twenty-five years or so. It now covers an area of about four square miles and embraces villages and communities which were once considered to be 'in the country', housing perhaps a third of the total population of the island. It also includes the deep water port facilities at the outer end of the peninsula which extends westwards into the middle of the harbour. The port is the first part of Antigua seen by about one third of all the visitors to the island. These arrive in the two hundred or more cruise ships which call each year. Although very few of these ships remain in port for more than one day their passengers add greatly to the life of St John's and to the economy of the country. During the months from November to May, when Caribbean cruising is most popular, the presence of two (and sometimes four or more) cruise ships in the harbour at the same time has an immediate impact on St John's. The main shopping streets are filled with tourists of all ages and speaking a variety of languages. The shopkeepers, taxi-drivers, tour bus operators and restauranteurs do thriving business, and the city becomes almost vibrant with noise and activity.

One regrettable feature of modern life and the supremacy of air travel is that it is now virtually impossible to travel between the Caribbean islands by sea, other than in a cruise ship or a yacht. There is constant movement of small coasters between the islands but it is extremely difficult to find one prepared to carry passengers. Very few visitors therefore, other than cruise ship passengers and yachtsmen, will arrive in Antigua via St John's Harbour.

St John's Harbour

Until the end of the 1960s all ships bigger than the local inter-island craft had to anchor well outside the harbour. Freight was then transferred into lighters before being unloaded into warehouses around

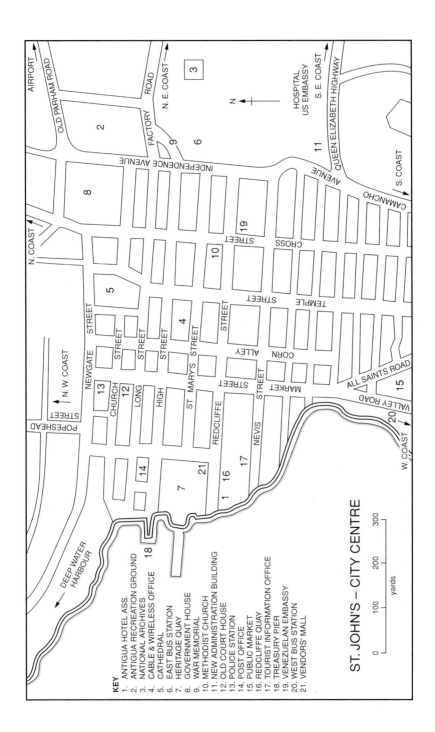

KEY
1. ANTIGUA HOTEL ASS.
2. ANTIGUA RECREATION GROUND
3. NATIONAL ARCHIVES
4. CABLE & WIRELESS OFFICE
5. CATHEDRAL
6. EAST BUS STATION
7. HERITAGE QUAY
8. GOVERNMENT HOUSE
9. WAR MEMORIAL
10. METHODIST CHURCH
11. NEW ADMINISTRATION BUILDING
12. OLD COURT HOUSE
13. POLICE STATION
14. POST OFFICE
15. PUBLIC MARKET
16. REDCLIFFE QUAY
17. TOURIST INFORMATION OFFICE
18. TREASURY PIER
19. VENEZUELAN EMBASSY
20. WEST BUS STATION
21. VENDORS' MALL

ST. JOHN'S – CITY CENTRE

0   100   200   300
        yards

the harbour, while passengers were brought ashore in launches to a small pier at the lower end of the city's main street. All this changed in 1968 following the construction of the present deep water port on the northern side of the harbour, at the outer end of a small islet, Rat Island, linked to the mainland by a causeway. By using a channel which was dredged through the sand bar across the mouth of the harbour, ships up to 600 feet in length, and drawing up to 30 feet of water, can now use the port. The largest vessels handled are cruise ships, and the Port Authority gives precedence to these in making berths available at the wharf. Their passengers can disembark within about thirty minutes of the ship's arrival alongside.

Once ashore the passengers find a tourist information desk inside the port administration building, through which they have to pass in order to leave the port. Immediately outside is a large shopping plaza with souvenir shops, bars and snack counters. International telephone facilities are also available. Taxis into the city, to nearby beaches, or for various island-wide tours, are obtained from a stand situated between the port building and the shopping plaza.

The road from the port into St John's crosses the original Rat Island causeway, now considerably widened. At the outer end, nestling up against the eastern end of Rat Island itself, is Antigua's only rum distillery. This produces the island's well-known 'Cavalier' rum. For anyone interested in the processes of its production a tour of the distillery can be arranged at reasonably short notice by contacting the manager (telephone 480-3210). Those who are more interested in sampling the product need travel no further than the nearest bar, hotel or restaurant. Rum, which has been termed 'the elixir of the islands', comes in many varieties, and there must be at least a hundred different kinds throughout the Caribbean. While it may not be totally true to claim that Antigua's particular brand actually prolongs life, it certainly has excellent restorative qualities and no visitor who is not a teetotaller should leave the island without sampling it.

A little further along the road between the port and the city centre there still remains the chance to see local craftsmen at work in a small boatyard, the last of several which used to line the northern side of the harbour. Up until the beginning of the 1980s it was not unusual to find perhaps half a dozen wooden boats of differing sizes, in various stages of completion, alongside the road. Regardless of size they were all built to a fairly standard design, without reference to any drawings and mostly with the use of hand tools. At the same time in the harbour behind them would have been seen some of the finished products at anchor, with the same high, raked bows, the thick, stumpy mast, and the after deck-house repeated in craft from under 30 to over 70 feet in length. Today, while the odd working boat still appears from time to time in the harbour, only repair work is carried out in the last functioning boatyard. It seems most unlikely that any new wooden boats of the traditional type will ever be built again in Antigua.

In the city the Old Treasury Pier, where all passengers landed in days gone by, remains in being and is gently falling into decay at the foot of High Street. A short distance away to the south is a much longer and far more substantial jetty, built in the late 1980s as part of a major harbour development scheme, which provides berths for two more cruise ships. Their passengers have a quite different introduction to the island from those who land at the commercial port, stepping ashore within a few yards of the city centre.

The city centre

The central area of St John's, containing the main shopping streets, banks and commercial institutions, is more or less confined to the limits of the original 18th century town. It appears today, allowing for changes in methods of transportation, still very much as it was described in the 1840s by Mrs Lanaghan:

The town, which is well arranged, covers a space of about 150 acres of land: most of the streets are wide and well-kept, and intersect each other at right angles – the principal ones running in a straight line down to the sea. There is one peculiarity attending the construction of these streets, which is, that there are no causeways; and consequently the pedestrian traveller has to elbow his way amid trucks and handbarrows, gigs, carriages and horsemen ...

At the corners of the different streets are seated hucksters ... some with their shallow trays, containing cakes of all descriptions, parched ground nuts, sugar cakes, and other confections, and varieties of fruit and vegetables; others have piles of cottons, coloured calicos, bright-tinted handkerchiefs, etc, placed by them, or carefully spread along the sides of the most frequented streets, to attract the eye of the passer-by.

While the street scenes may not have changed too much since her day, a resurrected Mrs Lanaghan would be hard pressed to recognize

69

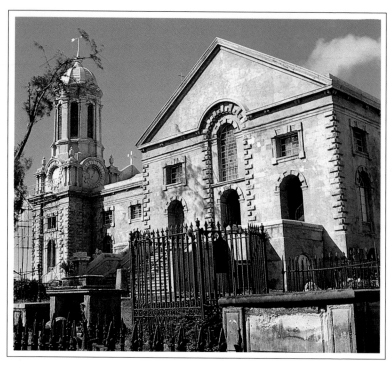

The Cathedral Church of St John the Divine (MICHAEL BOURNE)

anything else in the city other than one or two of the older public buildings. Until perhaps fifteen or even ten years ago this would not have been the case. St John's then still contained some fine examples of early and mid-nineteenth century architecture, and retained much charm and individuality, with many private houses even along the main streets. Much of its character has now been swept away in a prolonged orgy of demolition and rebuilding, taking most of the private dwellings with it. Concrete buildings, multi-storey office blocks, the garish facades of fast food franchises, a built-up waterfront, traffic lights (which may or may not work), and above all the motor-car, may have brought the city firmly into the twentieth century; but much of its attraction as a place to live and work has gone for ever.

Be this as it may, almost everything needed by the visitor in the way of goods and services, as well as cheap accommodation in small hotels and guest-houses, can be found in 'down-town' St John's which is more or less the area of the original town as Mrs Lanaghan

Shops at Redcliffe Quay, built around a pleasant shady courtyard
(MICHAEL BOURNE)

knew it. All the main places of historical interest are there and within easy walking distance of each other. The main shopping precincts, with one exception, are even closer together, being grouped around the head of the inner harbour cruise ship berths.

Shopping

Shopping in St John's has improved at the same rate as its charm and character have been eroded, and there are now stores of every size and description with an enormous choice of goods. These range from locally produced souvenirs to European china, crystal, perfumes and leatherware, South American gems and jewellery, Japanese electronic equipment, and liquor from the four corners of the world. The number of places selling clothing, from every conceivable pattern of tee-shirt to very expensive designer fashions, is legion, with boutiques in every street and stalls on every sidewalk. (The street seller has been part of city life since well before Mrs Lanaghan's day, and the creation of a Vendors' Mall at the lower end of Redcliffe Street in an attempt to clear some of the sidewalks promises to be no more than a palliative.) The local goods and handicrafts on sale include ceramic ware, wooden carvings and *Warri* boards, straw and basket work, and costume jewellery made from coral, shells and polished stones. Local artists display their work in small galleries or even on street corners.

Duty-free shopping is available at Heritage Quay, a large double-storey complex at the seaward end of St Mary's Street, and also in the adjoining Redcliffe Quay. The latter, an attractive grouping of shops, offices and eating places around a very pleasant courtyard, was created out of a collection of disused decrepit warehouses, and provides a good example of the sort of restoration work which might well have been emulated elsewhere in the city before the concrete mixers moved in. Shoppers wanting to make duty-free purchases need to present a passport and travel documents (or a landing pass if from a cruise ship).

The major out-of-town shopping precinct is Woods Shopping Mall, about one mile to the north-east of the city centre. This, besides having plenty of parking space (something which is at a premium within the city centre), has a post office and a whole array of stores, with many of the latter staying open until 9.00 pm.

Business hours

The normal business and commercial life of the city until a few years ago was between 8.00 am and 4.00 pm from Monday to Friday, but this has changed considerably. Many shops now open from 9.00 am until 5.00 pm from Monday to Saturday, or very similar hours, and the old colonial legacy of an 'early closing day' has all but disappeared.

Banking hours, however, remain much as they were in colonial days: from 8.00 am to 2.00 pm from Monday to Thursday, and on Fridays from 8.00 am to noon and from 3.00 to 5.00 pm.

The main Post Office, at the lower (western) end of High Street, is open daily from Monday to Friday between 8.00 am and 4.00 pm and on Saturday from 8.00 am to noon. Antigua and Barbuda issues many (for the pedantic philatelist probably too many) interesting and colourful postage stamps each year, and sets for collectors are available from the Philatelic Bureau in the Post Office.

Food and drink

Antigua is not renowned for its cuisine. There are no local dishes or foods which cannot be found in many other West Indian islands, even though these are perhaps prepared or served in slightly different ways. This is not to say that the local food is without interest or attraction. While 'kiddie (goat meat) stew' or 'shark quiche' (recipes for both of which are given in local cookery books) may not have more than minority appeal, there are many dishes which the visitor would be well advised to sample, given the opportunity. In St John's there are several restaurants which serve a variety of local dishes as alternatives to the ubiquitous hamburgers, steaks and 'french fries' of the average tourist-orientated menu. The visitor should have little difficulty in finding them, as they all advertise widely and are well sign-posted. No attempt is made here to indicate the specialities or attractions of any of them. The would-be patron is advised to seek local opinion about their relative merits as one good way of getting to know Antiguans.

Some of the dishes to look out for are:

Souse This is boiled pork (pig's head, knuckles or some other cut) marinated in water and lime-juice with onions, hot and sweet peppers, garlic and cucumber. It is usually served with lettuce and tomatoes and eaten with hot bread rolls.

An extensive shopping plaza at Heritage Quay, adjacent to the cruise ships
(MICHAEL BOURNE)

Salt fish   This is the traditional Antiguan Sunday morning breakfast dish. It is dried cod which has been soaked, boiled and boned, in a rich onion and tomato sauce. As a breakfast dish it is usually served with crushed aubergines (known locally as 'antrobers'). If eaten as a midday meal it is usually accompanied by doucouna.

Doucouna   This is a small pudding of grated sweet potato and coconut mixed together with flour and spices and boiled in a banana leaf.

Pepper Pot   This is a rich, thick stew containing salt beef, pork, pumpkin, paw-paw, spinach, peas, aubergines and okras, with onion, garlic and spices. It can be served with dumplings or with a cornmeal pudding known as **Fungee**. Since 1994 this has been recognized as the Antiguan national dish.

Conch Stew   Another excellent stew prepared with the large shellfish called conch. The meat has to be tenderised before being cooked with onions, tomatoes and spices, but if done properly the result is delicious.

Although Antigua's cuisine may fail to excite the gourmet, the range of vegetables available to supplement the more international fare of the hotels and restaurants is very wide and well worth his attention. Besides those mentioned above, the island also produces corn, carrots, beans, yams, squash, eddoes, christophenes, cassava, dasheen, avocado pears, breadfruit and plantains. Once again, as with the local fruit, modern catering methods and the trend towards a stereotyped 'international' menu will prevent many of these from being offered in the average restaurant or hotel dining room. The hotel guest or restaurant customer who does find things such as fried aubergine, paw-paw au gratin, pumpkin fritters, candied sweet potato or scalloped plantain on the menu will know that she has chosen well.

With regard to drinks, once again Antigua has no speciality or concoction peculiar to the island. Rum has already been mentioned and there can be few tourists who are not familiar – at least by name – with the more popular cocktails and mixtures which use rum as a base. Around Christmas time a deep red, non-alcoholic drink called **Sorrel** is prepared from the dried sepals of the sorrel flower. This is sweet and refreshing, and should never be refused if offered. The island grows plenty of lime trees and fresh limes are available at most times of the year. A lime squash made with fresh lime juice is an excellent thirst-quencher. Any attempt to serve a lime squash made from a commercially-bottled concentrate, which tastes totally different, should be rejected out of hand.

Places of interest

In recent years the change in appearance of St John's, brought about by the erection of numerous large and undistinguished buildings quite out of keeping with the size of the city, the width of the streets or anything else, has been offset slightly by the careful renovation of some of the older structures. **Redcliffe Quay** has already been mentioned, and a former residence in Nevis Street has been given a new lease of life as the offices of the Cultural Development Department. In nearby St Mary's Street the **central Methodist church**, which was badly damaged by an earthquake in 1974, has also been lovingly repaired and restored to its original condition. Surrounded by well-kept lawns and with an imposing row of royal palms on the southern side it is just as Mrs Lanaghan described it soon after it was built, ' ... an excellent building, superior to anything of the kind I have seen in the West Indies, and makes a good and commanding outward appearance, particularly when lighted up of an evening ...'.

When these words were written, before the advent of the high-rise office block on Antiguan soil, the building which used to dominate the city had not yet been built. This is the **Cathedral Church of St John the Divine**, set on a rise near the north-eastern end of the central part of the city. Besides being the mother church of the Anglican Diocese of the North Eastern Caribbean and Aruba, it is also considered to be a national monument with a meaning for the whole community. It is one of the most imposing of all the Anglican cathedrals in the West Indies; although when first built it was thought by one intemperate English ecclesiologist to resemble nothing more than 'a pagan temple with two dumpty pepper-pot towers'. Having been erected in 1847, it has had to withstand a number of earthquakes and hurricanes and is in constant need of repair and restoration work, for which there are never sufficient funds. The cathedral is built of cement-washed stone but the interior is completely encased in pine to lessen the effects of damage by earthquake or hurricane. It can seat about two thousand people and congregations of this size are seen from time to time on State occasions or when a service is attended by royalty or high Anglican dignitaries. The life-sized metal figures on the pillars of the south gates to the churchyard were

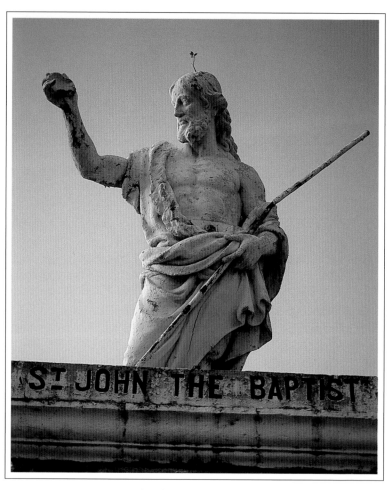

St John the Baptist (CHRIS HUXLEY)

erected in 1789. They represent St John the Baptist and St John the Divine, and it is probable that they were taken from a French ship captured during the Seven Years War of 1756–63.

The oldest building still in use in St John's is the **Old Court House** at the junction of Long Street and Market Street. It was built in 1747 of stone quarried from one of the small islands off the north coast. Although it has been damaged, rebuilt and restored on several occasions since, it still retains much of its original appearance. Once again the description given in *Antigua and the Antiguans* serves very well for today.

The court house is a very noble-looking pile for a West India colony, and indeed would not disgrace the boasted streets of London. The plan of the structure is very uniform and neat ...

The principal entrance (to the south) is approached by iron gates; and after crossing a small court-yard paved with large flagstones, you enter a small corridor, supported by circular stone columns, with plain capitals. At each end of this corridor, a flight of stairs leads to the upper apartments in the east and west wings ...

The building now houses the **Museum of Antigua and Barbuda**. This contains displays covering every period of the prehistory and history of the two islands, as well as a considerable collection of curiosities ranging from Arawak artefacts to Second World War uniforms and Viv Richards' cricket bat. The museum is a relatively new institución which affords the visitor a fascinating, if somewhat whimsical, look at the history of the islands. The long period that Antigua spent as a colony must be taken as the reason for any deficiencies in the museum's contents. Many of the more important and valuable items of the type normally found in a national museum have long since left the island, or simply been allowed to deteriorate in the hands of those not conscious of their historical interest.

For some years the upper floor housed the country's archives, but these are now stored in a purpose-built **National Archives Building** about a third of a mile to the east of the museum. Adjacent to this in an area known as Victoria Park are the **Botanical Gardens**. These were created as long ago as 1893 and were well looked after for the next fifty or sixty years, before being allowed to deteriorate during the fairly turbulent period after the Second World War. Nothing much was done about this until the late 1980s when a Botanic Society was formed in order to attempt their restoration. A considerable amount of work had been done by the time that centennial celebrations were held in 1993. Since then more has been achieved, and the gardens are now once again worth visiting.

On the opposite side of the archives building to the botanical gardens is a large walled sports field called the **Antigua Recreation Ground**. Since 1981 this has been a recognised venue for cricket Test matches. (A 'Test' match is a game in a 'Test series', played between teams representing countries which belong to the International Cricket Conference.) Any visitor who is in Antigua while one of these matches is being played is advised to see at least one day's play. Cricket is the game which has been described as a dramatic spectacle more akin to the theatre, ballet and the dance than a mere sporting activity. It is one which is closely linked with England and the English way of life; but has been mastered in no mean fashion by West Indians.

It is possible to argue (and many have done so: just as a game of cricket takes longer to play than any other, commentators on the game tend to be the most long-winded and dogmatic of sports writers) that no one from a non-cricket playing country can understand the finer points of the game (and for the uninitiated there are many …). This will not prevent anyone from getting a lot of enjoyment from watching a Test match in Antigua. Fellow spectators will be voluble, knowledgeable and above all friendly. There will be much noise, colour and amusement, and a great deal of entertainment from the players and onlookers alike. In addition the setting for such a game is superb. Despite its rather pedestrian name the Antigua Recreation Ground is in surroundings at least equal in attractiveness to Test match grounds with more appealing names, such as the Queen's Park Oval in Port of Spain or Sabina Park in Kingston. The ground is almost surrounded by trees and the lovely view through and over them to the south from the main stands adds greatly to the overall spectacle.

Carnival

The annual carnival is the most popular cultural event in the island, appealing to visitors as much as it does to Antiguans. It takes place at the end of July, lasting for about ten days and ending with national holidays on the first Monday and Tuesday in August. It originated as a form of Christmas celebration. In days gone by, from Christmas Eve until New Year's Day, revellers took to the streets in weird costumes made from dried banana and other leaves, dressed as ghosts, or walking on stilts. After 1957, when the first summer carnival was held, these winter activities soon disappeared and Christmas in Antigua is now very much as in any other part of the world. The summer carnival was modelled on the much bigger and more famous Trinidad Carnival, with steel bands leading troupes called 'Mas bands' through the streets. Each troupe had its own theme with the members (who 'play Mas') dressed to depict things like 'The Glory of Ancient Rome', 'Aztecs', 'Mexicans' or 'Flags of Siena'. In later years they chose more topical or symbolic themes – 'Space People', 'Bird People', 'Our African Heritage' and the like. Today the emphasis is on fantasy or historical themes.

For the first five years after 1957, Carnival remained a purely local event, consisting of the street festivities together with a Carnival Queen contest and a calypso competition. In 1962 a Caribbean Queen contest was introduced which has since become the highlight of the many shows, attracting contestants from all parts of the West Indies. Today the Antigua Carnival embraces the Caribbean and local Queen contests, calypso and steel band competitions, a 'Miss Teenage Pageant', a junior calypso competition and a junior carnival. All these events are staged in 'Carnival City', in an outdoor arena created for the occasion on a sports field, but a great deal of carnival activity goes on in other parts of St John's as well.

The original 1957 calypso competition had seven competitors for the title of 'Calypso King'; today the number is likely to be seventy or more. The final contestants are chosen from among the winners of preliminary competitions which are held in several 'calypso tents' around the city, established well before the opening of Carnival City. Steel bands made their appearance in Antigua shortly after the end of the Second World War. There was much local opposition at the time to 'pan men' and their music. This was overcome with the support of Lord Baldwin, a benevolent British Governor of the late 1940s. The unique sound of the steel band (now of course synonymous with the West Indies) has been heard in Antigua ever since. Each band taking part in the competition has its own 'pan yard' in which to tune up and practise, and naturally in the period leading up to carnival these are in constant use.

The noise and general excitement begin well before the official ten-day period of carnival, but reach a climax on the morning of the first Monday in August, in what is known as *Jouve* or *J'ouvert* (a cor-ruption of *jour ouvert*). This is when the main streets of St John's are jammed with people marching, shuffling and dancing ('jumping up') to the music of steel bands and amplified sound systems. The proces-sion begins at four o'clock in the morning and continues for perhaps four or five hours until the sun is well overhead. St John's then closes its shutters and the streets remain deserted until mid-afternoon. This

Carnival (overleaf) (CHRIS HUXLEY)

is the time when the costumed 'mas bands' parade through the town on their way to the stage in Carnival City for judging. The stalwart 'masquerader' will continue his enjoyment throughout that night and the following day, ending with a final street 'jump up' at 'Las lap' on Tuesday afternoon. By the time this ends the streets will be partially blocked by the huge steel trolleys on which the steel bands have performed, littered with the colourful remains of abandoned carnival costumes, and it will be all too apparent that Carnival is over for yet another year.

All roads lead to St John's ...

Anyone spending some time in St John's is bound to see that there are some areas which look dilapidated and in urgent need of restoration – but no more and no less than in any other capital city. These parts are more than compensated for by the many well-maintained and brightly painted shops and commercial buildings, interspersed with eating places set in secluded courtyards surrounded and overhung by shady tropical shrubs and trees. During the weekdays the main streets are filled with activity and St John's is clearly the centre of life on the island. The main roads radiate from it, the airport is but four miles away, the main port is an integral part of it, and a good many people from the outlying villages come in daily to work in or around the city. At the weekend and especially on Sunday it is different. The streets are then twice as wide, with fewer parked cars. The few private dwellings with their doors and windows open stand out from the shuttered shops and offices. The inner part of the harbour with yachts and boats at anchor, seen at the lower end of the main east-west streets, seems to be much more part of the town. Under such circumstances the atmosphere of St John's almost reverts to that of another era, one which existed before the introduction of traffic lights and the advent of multi-storey buildings.

While to stay in a small hotel or guest-house in the capital may not be everyone's idea of a Caribbean vacation, the changing moods of the place – from cosmopolitan city to old-fashioned town – will have their appeal. This type of accommodation may also be an attractive proposition for someone planning to hike or travel by bus around the island. The prosaically named East and West Bus Stations are less than half a mile apart on opposite sides of the city centre. The East Bus Station is used by buses carrying passengers to villages to the

Traditional town buildings in St John's <small>(MICHAEL BOURNE)</small>

north and east, and the West Bus Station by those servicing the central, south and west communities.

Because St John's is the focus of the island's road network, and there is no road which follows all the way around the coast, anyone wishing to visit any part of the island is almost bound to take the city as a starting point. The next four chapters give a description of Antigua, working in a clockwise direction from St John's. The route of a suggested tour is indicated on the map which accompanies each chapter.

DEVELOPED ANTIGUA

Prickly Pear Island

Great Bird Island

Long Island

FERRY

Maiden Island

Rabbit Island

CRABBS PENINSULA

Guiana Island

Beggars Point
Jabberwock Beach
Antigua Defence Force
US Airforce Station

Marina

St George's Church

Rat Island

PARHAM HARBOUR

Parham

St Peter's Church

AIRPORT

Piggotts

Cedar Grove

Barnes Hill

New Winthorpes

Cedar Valley Golf Club

St Johnston Village

Potters

Oil Refinery

ST JOHN'S

The Sisters

DICKENSON BAY

Oil Jetty

RUNAWAY BAY

FORT BAY

Fort James

0   1   2   3

Miles

84

| 9 |
Developed Antigua

The northern part of Antigua, that area to the north of a line drawn between St John's and Parham, is where the main development of the island has taken place in modern times. It contains not only the airport and the main sea port, together with the majority of Antiguan industries, but also well over half of all the visitor accommodation available on the island. There is also a lot of residential development, ranging from low-cost Government housing estates to expensive private houses set in their own landscaped grounds. As might be expected there is an extensive road network in this part of the island, including a road around most of the coastline. While much of the coast, away from the stretch facing the north-west, has no particular merit, some of the views to seaward – especially over North Sound – are very fine. A tour around the northern coast is recommended for these as much as the opportunity to see something of modern Antigua before venturing further afield.

The north-west coast, between the entrance to St John's Harbour and **Boon Point** (the northernmost point of Antigua), is undoubtedly the main tourist area on the island. It has three of the finest beaches. Two of them are lined with hotels, condominium developments, guest-houses and beach cottages, mixed with a few restaurants and beach bars, and there are other hotels and eating places a little way inland. The actual coastline remains attractive and relatively unspoiled. None of the buildings is obtrusive and they are all set in well-landscaped surroundings with plenty of palms and flowering shrubs. A little way inland, a couple of miles to the north-east of St John's, is the island's only 18-hole golf course at the **Cedar Valley Golf Club**. This offers full facilities to visiting golfers. The third beach, behind which no development has taken place as yet, is the one closest to St John's. Called Fort Bay, it begins in the south at Fort James.

Fort James and Fort Bay

To reach **Fort James**, situated on the promontory which forms the northern entrance point of St John's Harbour, leave the city by the

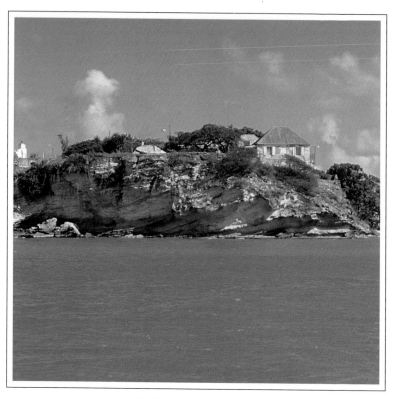

Fort James (PADDY BROWNE)

aptly named Fort Road and continue northwards to the **Barrymore Hotel**. Turn left at the hotel and continue along the road until it reaches the sea. The road then runs parallel to the beach until it ends at the fort. Built in the first half of the 18th century to guard the harbour, Fort James had accommodation for about seventy men. The guns they were to man were never very many, and were never fired in anger. Perhaps because of this lack of action a custom grew up whereby the officer commanding the fort began to extract dues from ships using the harbour. This practice, of dubious legality, was greatly resented by the local ship-owners but seems to have continued until well into the 19th century. The walls are still in excellent condition and a few of the cannon remain in place, but the main attraction of a visit is the excellent view it affords of the harbour and its approaches.

The beach in **Fort Bay** is equally excellent. It has long been the local beach for the residents of St John's and a few inhabitants swim there each morning throughout the year. There is a small beach bar at the southern end, and a much larger one – well patronised by cruise ship passengers – towards the northern end. This is a popular beach with Antiguans on public holidays, particularly on Labour Day; but for most of the year, away from the immediate environs of the larger beach bar, it is unusual to find more than one or two dozen people along its whole length.

Runaway Bay and Dickenson Bay

The next beach to the north, in **Runaway Bay**, will probably have a few more people using it on the average day as it is lined with tourist accommodation of one sort or another. The buildings stand on a narrow strip of land separating the sea from one of the large salt ponds. The structure in the sea about a mile offshore is a jetty used for the transfer of oil fuel. It is connected by an underwater pipeline to the storage tanks which form part of the disused oil refinery on the inland side of the salt pond. The pond, which is called McKinnons, has a large population of migratory shore birds, terns, plovers and herons, in the fall. The road between it and the beach leads to the southern end of the next bay.

The beach in **Dickenson Bay** is the most popular of the three on this coast. There are two large hotels, with other accommodation in a condominium development and in various beach apartments. The beach also supports several restaurants and water sports' centres. The bay provides ideal conditions for board-sailing, water-skiing and snorkeling, as well as very safe swimming conditions on a gently shelving beach. While it is understandably popular, the beach is never overcrowded.

Dickenson Bay is also used as the starting point, or a pick-up point, for a number of boat tours. These include a 'pirate cruise' to Deep Bay (see Chapter 12) in a large wooden schooner called the *Jolly Roger*, a complete circumnavigation of Antigua, and several tours in smaller sailing craft to one or other of the islets off the north-east coast. All these cruises include substantial meals with seemingly endless drinks, and combine a great deal of enjoyment with the opportunity of seeing something of the island from seaward. The necessary arrangements are easily made through the hotels or individual booking offices in St John's. At least one glass-bottomed boat is operated from the bay, offering various trips to the reefs off the north

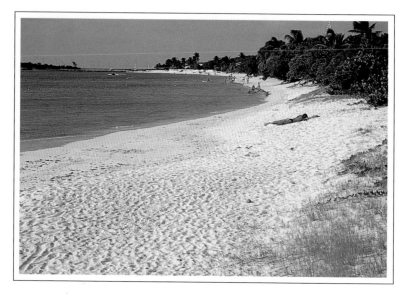

Runaway Beach (CHRIS HUXLEY)

coast or to Great Bird Island, the most popular picnic site amongst the islets further to the east.

The north coast

The road around the north coast from Dickenson Bay crosses Marble Hill and then runs parallel to the coast about half a mile inland to the village of Cedar Grove. From there it follows the coastline to the airport. The area between Boon Point and Beggars Point is of no great interest to the visitor, being almost entirely residential and with no access to the one or two small beaches. About half a mile off Beggars Point is a very small treeless islet called **Prickly Pear Island**. This has a very fine beach on its western side which is used frequently for picnic and beach parties. Scheduled trips from a landing place on Beggars Point operate during the winter tourist season. The beach to the south of Beggars Point and immediately alongside the road is known locally as the **Jabberwock Beach** after a night-club of that name which, until it was demolished many years ago, used to form part of a hotel in the vicinity. The beach offers good bathing and snorkeling under normal conditions, but occasionally the prevailing wind can stir up waves which make it unsafe for children.

The road meanders inland from the southern end of Jabberwock Beach around the fenced perimeter of what was, for over fifty years, a US Naval Facility. The land which this occupied, and which formed only a small part of the total leased to the USA by the British Government in 1941, was returned to Antiguan jurisdiction only in the early 1990s. The facility now houses **Camp Blizzard** (named after an old estate in the area) and contains the headquarters of the Antigua and Barbuda Defence Force. It is adjacent to a small US Air Force Base which opened in 1957 as a missile and satellite tracking station, but which now functions as a tracking station and communications centre. This now occupies only a tiny portion of the total area leased to the United States during the Second World War, and which then included all the land occupied by the present airport.

The V C Bird International Airport has been constructed on the same site as the first airstrip, then called Coolidge Air Field, which was laid down by the then US Army Air Force in 1941. It retained this name (that of a First World War hero, Captain Hamilton Coolidge of the US Army Air Corps who was killed over France in 1918) until 1985.

The road around the airport passing Barnacle Point provides splendid views across Parham Sound to Long Island, Maiden Island and Crabbs Peninsula. On the southern side of the airport, after passing a large quarry, the road divides, with the left-hand track leading to **St George's church** on Fitches Creek Bay. This is an Anglican church built in 1687, but remodelled into its present form fifty years later. It has been much restored in recent years. Despite modern houses built nearby it retains its historic appeal in a quiet, rural setting which exudes peace and tranquility. It contains the tomb of William Barnes, the first English settler to have his remains interred within a place of worship, and who died aged 34 only eight years after the original church was built.

Parham, Crabbs Peninsula and North Sound

From St George's church an unpaved road leads around the head of Fitches Creek Bay and continues into the town of **Parham**, one of the original settlements of the 17th century. Because one of the early Governors lived there a common misconception has arisen that Parham was the original capital of Antigua. This was never the case, and although Parham used to be a port it never rivalled St John's. There is still a small pier at the eastern end of the town, and Parham Harbour provides a well-protected anchorage for yachts and small fishing boats, but there is no evidence of any other port facilities. The most prominent building in the town is **St Peter's Anglican Church**. This was built in 1842 and is octagonal in shape. With its splendid proportions and its unique wooden ceiling, it is considered to be one of the finest examples of Georgian colonial architecture to be found in the West Indies.

Crabbs Peninsula, which is low and flat, forms the eastern side of Parham Harbour. During the Second World War it was leased to the USA and housed a US Naval Air Station and a US Marine Corps Camp. Today it is the site for, among other things, a small yacht marina and boat yard. The outer end of the peninsula is a restricted area used by the Antigua Defence Force. **Long Island**, about two miles away, belongs to the **Jumby Bay Resort**. A private ferry service is operated from a point on the mainland near the **Beachcomber Hotel**. Casual visitors are welcomed, provided arrangements are made with the management beforehand. The island is one of the places known to have been inhabited by both the pre-historic Ciboney people, in around 500 BC, and the Arawaks around 1500 years later. An archaeological site has been investigated on the north coast. In colonial times the island was a private estate mainly used for raising cattle.

On the eastern side of Crabbs Peninsula, and separated from the mainland by The Narrows, a stretch of water about four hundred feet wide, is the largest of Antigua's off-lying islands. **Guiana Island** acquired its name from its first settlers. These were some Englishmen who had been forced to leave Dutch Guiana (now Surinam) in 1667, after the Treaty of Breda left that country in Dutch hands. Originally it was planted with sugar cane, but under subsequent owners it became a shooting estate. During the years between the First and Second World Wars it was turned into a park, with avenues of trees, coconut groves and immense shrubberies and flower beds. In recent years it has been allowed to return to its natural state and is now a Nature Reserve, with a herd of deer and a flock of prize sheep. It is also a protected habitat of Guinea-fowl, wild ducks and other birds. A pontoon bridge connects it to the mainland, but there is no public access.

To the north of Guiana Island and lying amidst numerous patches of coral reef are several other, much smaller, islands. The largest,

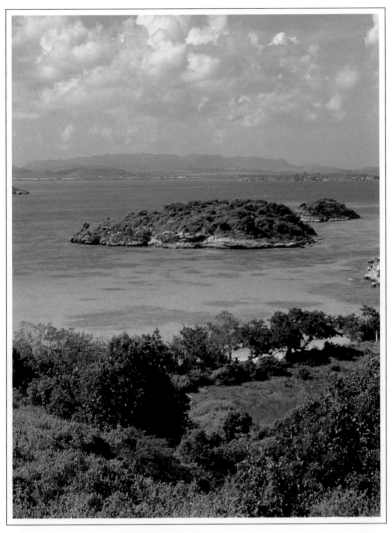

Great Bird Island (PADDY BROWNE)

called **Great Bird Island**, is very popular with picnicking and swimming parties. It provides an ideal overnight anchorage for yachts on the western side. The eastern side of the island is an eroded limestone cliff nearly a hundred feet high. This provides good nesting for seabirds, and a spectacular view of the surrounding reefs from the top. In recent years, through the increasing number of visitors, it has been discovered that the island is the last remaining habitat of what may well be the world's rarest snake, the Antigua racer (*Alsophis antiguae*). This is a harmless grass snake, which grows to about three feet in length, and of which there are probably no more than about 150 still in existence. Although a captive breeding programme has been initiated, and the island is very much under the eye of the local conservation organisation, it remains to be seen whether the snake will continue to be able to cope with the increasing number of visitors who tramp through its habitat each year.

| 10 |
Remote Antigua

The eastern part of the island is reached from St John's by a road running past the disused Gunthorpe's sugar factory towards the villages of Pares and Glanvilles. The factory was built in the early years of the twentieth century and began operating in 1905. Its opening was a major event in the life of ordinary Antiguans of the day, leading to the beginning of technical training for some workers and eventually to the introduction of trade unionism into the island. The amount of sugar produced each year varied enormously but occasionally reached over 20 000 tons. The factory was shut down in 1971 and, despite an attempt to reactivate it in the 1980s, has remained closed ever since.

Just to the south of the road between Pares and Glanvilles, but not seen from it, are the ruins of **Betty's Hope** estate, one of the largest of the original sugar plantations. The estate, which was founded (the word 'hope' being used in its now archaic sense of an enclosed piece of land) in about 1650, continued to be worked until the 1940s. From then on, until the late 1980s when a restoration project began, the complex of estate buildings – houses, factory and two windmills – was allowed to fall into total disrepair. Considerable clearing and restoration work has been completed and Betty's Hope is now a prime heritage monument. One of the windmills, dating from 1737, has been fully restored and is now complete with sails and crushing machinery. A nearby cotton storage house has been converted into an interpretation centre and the whole site, which is open every day except Sunday and Monday, is well worth the detour from the main road.

Mercers Creek Bay and Nonsuch Bay

In the early part of the last century Henry Coleridge in his book *Six Months in the West Indies* described the coastline of Antigua:

... indented in every direction with creeks and bays and coves, some of them running into the centre of the plantations like canals, some swelling into estuaries, and others forming spacious harbours.

Beyond these an infinite variety of islands and islets stud the bosom of the blue sea, and stand out like so many advanced posts of defence against the invading waves. They are of all shapes and sizes.

Allowing for the odd hyperbole, this description applies particularly to the eastern side of the island. **Mercers Creek Bay** is almost totally enclosed, with narrow openings to the sea between small islets lying across the entrance. The shoreline is divided into small coves and creeks by narrow spits of land. A good panoramic view of the bay can be obtained from the bluff on which the village of **Seatons** is built. This small detour from the main road between St John's and the north-eastern point of the island is well worth making. The main road itself passes through the village of Willikies and ends at **Long Bay**, where there is another excellent bathing beach with a hotel at either end. This beach is very popular with Antiguans. At the weekend during the summer months (many local people resolutely refuse to enter the sea between about November and March, although the sea temperature never varies by more than three degrees about a mean of 79 °F throughout the year) it may become a little crowded, but only in comparison to the normal conditions prevailing on Antiguan beaches.

Indian Town Point is the north-eastern extremity of the island. It is a low, flat area of mostly exposed and eroded limestone, reached by a track which passes through an arid stretch of countryside. This is probably the driest part of the whole island, as is borne out by the various species of cacti to be seen. The main attraction of the Point, other than the views of the Atlantic, is the natural limestone arch on the eastern side known as **Devil's Bridge**. This has been created by the action of the surf, and when the sea is running the formation of the arch produces some dramatic effects of waves and spray. Regardless of its name, Indian Town Point is not the location of any 'Indian' or pre-historic settlement, and the origin of the name is obscure. Some evidence of Arawak habitation has been found in this part of the island, but the lack of an adequate rainfall undoubtedly would have prevented any permanent settlement.

To the south of Indian Town Point is an irregular-shaped expanse of water called **Nonsuch Bay**. In spite of its general inaccessibility and lack of beaches, parts of its shoreline have begun to be developed in recent years. A resort called **Emerald Cove**, which is intended to incorporate its own golf course and marina, was started in

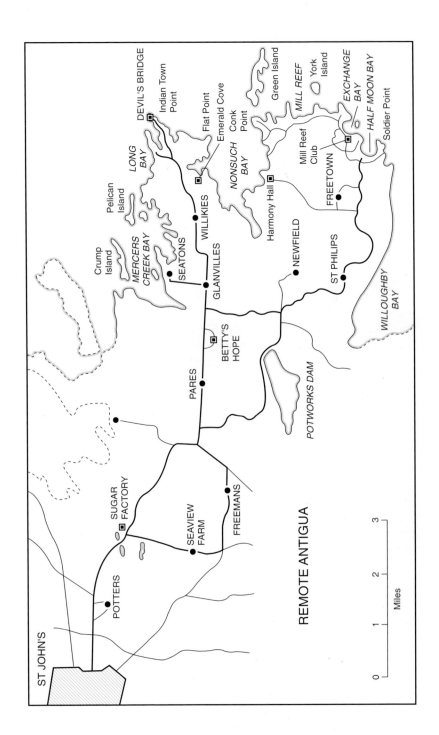

REMOTE ANTIGUA

ST JOHN'S

POTTERS

SUGAR FACTORY

SEAVIEW FARM

FREEMANS

PARES

BETTY'S HOPE

GLANVILLES

SEATONS

WILLIKIES

POTWORKS DAM

NEWFIELD

ST PHILIPS

CRUMP Island

MERCERS CREEK BAY

Pelican Island

LONG BAY

DEVIL'S BRIDGE

Indian Town Point

Flat Point

Emerald Cove

Conk Point

NONSUCH BAY

Green Island

MILL REEF

York Island

EXCHANGE BAY

HALF MOON BAY

Soldier Point

Mill Reef Club

FREETOWN

Harmony Hall

WILLOUGHBY BAY

Miles

0   1   2   3

Devil's Bridge (MICHAEL BOURNE)

the mid-1980s on the northern side, about halfway between Indian Town Point and the village of Willikies. The bay itself is popular with yachtsmen although it is not easy to get into from seaward. A large coral reef lies across the mouth protecting it from the Atlantic swells. The main entrance is through a narrow channel from the south which passes between the mainland and the small islet called Green Island. The only other entrance is through a tortuous channel between the reefs from the north. The bay is supposed to have been named after a ship, the Nonsuch, which anchored there for some time in 1647, presumably the first ever to do so.

Willoughby Bay and Half Moon Bay

To reach the area to the south of Nonsuch Bay from Indian Town Point it is necessary to return inland to the village of Glanvilles, and then take the road south to **St Philips**. This small village takes its name from the Anglican church which has been there since about 1690, and around which it grew up. It is built near the edge of the steep escarpment which forms the north shore of **Willoughby Bay**, and some superb views of the bay and the country on the opposite side are obtained at various points along the road which continues towards the east. The bay, although wide and deep, was never of any importance as a harbour as its entrance is almost completely blocked by coral reefs. Two miles on from St Philips a side road leads to the village of Freetown, and then on to the southern side of Nonsuch Bay. It eventually reaches an old estate house, now much restored and converted into an art gallery called **Harmony Hall**, before ending on the shore of the bay.

Half Moon Bay (MICHAEL BOURNE)

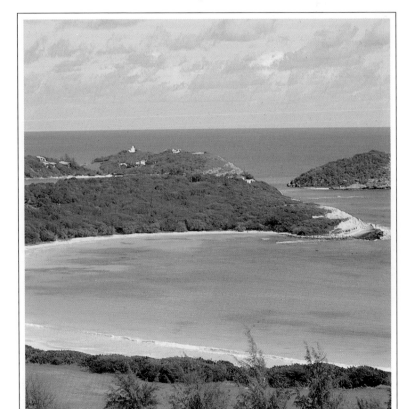

Half Moon Bay, where the main road ends to the south-east, is one of Antigua's major tourist attractions. Due to its almost circular shape, with the entrance facing the Atlantic swells, every kind of sea condition from crashing rollers to rippling wavelets is to be found at some point along the length of its beach, providing a wide variety of swimming conditions.

The area to the north of Half Moon Bay as far as the southern side of Nonsuch Bay, including all the small islands offshore, belongs to a proprietary club with limited membership, called the **Mill Reef Club**. This consists of a clubhouse on Exchange Bay and numerous elegant tropical houses scattered around its 1300 or so acres, together with a 9-hole golf course and a yacht harbour. The Club was started in 1948, and although some of Antigua's politicians and prominent citizens have been made honorary members, it was intended to be – and remains – an exclusive resort mainly for wealthy North Americans.

The creation of Mill Reef by an American architect so soon after the end of the Second World War helped to consolidate the connection between Antigua and the USA which the war had introduced. The construction work necessitated bringing an American building contractor to the island and created new employment opportunities. The requirements of the club members for goods and services of every kind helped to bring into being many new businesses, and introduced new American products and business methods to the island. Today Antigua benefits not only by the number of jobs provided by the club and the contribution the members make to the general revenue, but also from the charitable work carried out through the Mill Reef Fund, in the form of grants, donations and scholarships. The island also benefits from the free publicity it is given by the internationally known people who are members or guests of the club. In some circles, due to the foresight of its founder Mr 'Happy' Ward, Antigua is synonymous with the Mill Reef Club; just as in other circles, due to the prowess of Mr 'Vivi' Richards, it is synonymous with the game of cricket.

Potworks Dam and Sea View Farm

A visit to the east cost from St John's gives the opportunity of crossing the island by two different routes. It is suggested that the return trip is made via the island's main reservoir and two of the central villages. The reservoir which is always referred to as the **Potworks**

Dam was created in the late 1960s, and is fed by streams which flow into it during rainy weather. It is very shallow and during times of severe drought virtually dries out. The road along the north side passes over the dam proper and there is an observation point at the western end. The reservoir has no intrinsic value as a tourist attraction, as its setting in the flattest part of the island is very dull. However the bird life which it harbours will be of interest to the bird-watcher.

From the reservoir the visitor is recommended to follow a route which leads through the village of Freemans to another small community called **Sea View Farm**. This has an excellent view of the sea to the north and north-west, but the amount of farming activity carried on around it hardly justifies the name. It is far more renowned for its potteries, and several will be found along the road running through the village. (The visitor should not be misled by the much larger community about two miles to the north-west, which is called Potters Village, but where in fact there are no potteries.) The potters, who are all female, make mostly charcoal braziers ('coal pots'), cooking pots and plant pots intended for local use. They also produce a range of smaller items which many visitors find make good souvenirs. All the pottery is a distinctive deep red in colour, and is fired in open pits behind the potters' houses. A visit to one of these potteries, the inspection of the products, and the negotiations about prices, are all carried out in a very informal way. Such a visit will also provide another insight into the ordinary village way of life.

Return to St John's is completed by rejoining the main road near the sugar factory. If the city is then re-entered along the Queen Elizabeth Highway an unusual sculpture will be seen on one wall of the Administration Building found at the western end of the highway. The numerous flower pots which have been used in the construction of this, and a large fountain created at the time of the independence celebrations in 1981, were all made by the potters of Seaview Farm.

HISTORIC ANTIGUA

To
St John's

From
St John's

ALL SAINTS

POTWORKS
DAM

TABLE HILL
GORDON

BETHESDA

LIBERTA

CHRISTIAN
HILL

WILLOUGHBY
BAY

MONKS HILL
(Great George Fort)

FALMOUTH

COBBS CROSS

ENGLISH HARBOUR
TOWN

Falmouth
Harbour

NELSON'S
DOCKYARD

BAT'S CAVE

ST JAMES'S
CLUB

Blake
Island

CLARENCE HOUSE

MAMORA
BAY

MIDDLE
GROUND

DOW'S HILL

Proctors
Point

Standfast
Point

English
Harbour

Indian
Creek

FORT
BERKELEY

Nanton
Point

Cape
Shirley

FORT
SHIRLEY

THE
BLOCKHOUSE

0   1/2   1   2

Miles

| 11 |
Historic Antigua

The focal point of any visit to the south of the island must be English Harbour and its celebrated Dockyard. The harbour is one of the smaller indentations in the coastline of Antigua, but the security it has offered ships and boats throughout the island's history gives it an importance which far belies its size. The creation and development of a Naval Dockyard within the harbour had an effect on the whole of the surrounding countryside. Because of this there are several other aspects of this part of the island which are equally interesting and worth the visitor's attention.

Mrs Lanaghan described the road from St John's to English Harbour as, '... for the most part dull and uninteresting ... '. This was perhaps a little harsh; between the city and the outskirts of **Liberta** there is not much of interest; but after that, where the road winds over the hills, through Liberta and down to Falmouth, the scenery and views are most attractive. Neither need the journey be a dull one, provided the traveller has time to stop now and then to observe life in the villages and away from the road.

Monks Hill and Falmouth Harbour

At Liberta the road to **Monks Hill Fort** (properly called Great George Fort) is signposted. For those who wish to see one of Antigua's finest historical sites it is necessary to turn off the main road and head for the small village of **Table Hill Gordon**. From there it is about one mile to the fort. The track offers easy walking, but it is only motorable in a four wheel drive vehicle.

The fort, which was also intended to be a citadel in which non-combatants could take refuge, as well as a defensive position and signal station, was begun towards the end of the 17th century and completed in about 1705. The outer walls, which are more or less complete, embraced an area of over seven acres on which were built barracks, magazines, a hospital and two enormous cisterns. In the event it was never needed as a refuge, its guns were never fired, and after the end of the Napoleonic wars it soon fell into disuse except as

The Copper and Lumber Store at Nelson's Dockyard (MICHAEL BOURNE)

a signal station. This does not detract from the incredible setting of the fort on top of a steep-sided hill dominating Falmouth Harbour and the surrounding countryside. While it is nowhere near as big, and certainly not anywhere near in the same state of repair, as the similar structures of La Ferrière in Haiti or Brimstone Hill in St Kitts, the siting of Great George Fort is just as impressive. The views from it are equally spectacular.

The track from Table Hill Gordon leads to the only entrance, an arched doorway on the north side, and continues inside towards the eastern end. The whole of the fort is overgrown with acacia bushes and cacti, and all the buildings are in ruins. Nothing much can be seen of the surroundings until the higher ground at the eastern end is reached. There, by moving a few paces one way or the other around the circular stone structure which was once the base of a flagstaff, it is possible to see out in every direction. The southern side of Monks Hill is precipitous and from the top of the wall at the south-eastern extremity of the fort, nearly seven hundred feet above sea level, the view is truly magnificent. This alone, the panorama of Falmouth Harbour, English Harbour, and the large peninsula called Middle

Ground between them, makes the climb (or bumpy ride in a cross-country vehicle) very worthwhile. It is possible to descend by a track which leads down to the village of Cobbs Cross on Falmouth Harbour, but this is suitable only for walking.

Falmouth Harbour has been in use as a safe anchorage for ships since the earliest days, and Falmouth Town on the northern side was one of the first settlements. Today the village houses only a small community and any importance it had has long since been transferred across the bay to the town of English Harbour. The harbour itself remains very much in use, at times providing anchorages for as many yachts as English Harbour, from which it is separated by a narrowing isthmus. The road from St John's passes through Falmouth and Cobbs Cross before reaching English Harbour Town. There it divides, with the right-hand road leading to the Dockyard, and the left-hand one leading to the remains of the fortifications which used to guard it. It is recommended that the latter are visited first, in order to get an overall view of English Harbour and to place the Dockyard in its proper perspective.

Dow's Hill Historical Centre

Before reaching anything of interest the visitor is required to pay a Nelson's Dockyard National Park entrance fee. As well as covering access to all the fortifications, and the dockyard itself, this also permits entry into the **Dow's Hill Historical Centre**. This is a purpose-built complex on a hill to the north of the approach road, which provides an excellent multi-media presentation of the major aspects of Antigua's history and culture. Close to it, constructed on the foundations of a large house destroyed by earthquake in 1843, is the **Belvedere**; this is an observation platform with explanatory signboards, which provides a panoramic view of the entire National Park.

Shirley Heights

The extensive ruins of barracks, gun emplacements, magazines and other military buildings found all over the high ground to the south of Dow's Hill are generally referred to as **Shirley Heights**. From the Historical Centre the road runs along the crest of a ridge for about three quarters of a mile before dividing at a half-buried upright

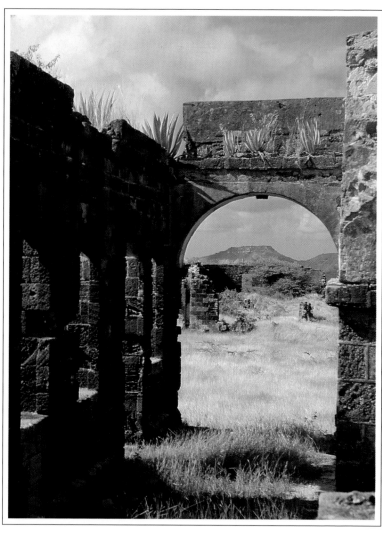

The ruined barracks at Shirley Heights (PADDY BROWNE)

cannon. The left-hand road continues to climb until it ends on top of the cliff which forms **Cape Shirley**, well over four hundred feet above sea level. The buildings in this vicinity formed **The Blockhouse**, and consisted of barracks, officers' quarters, a magazine and various domestic quarters. The battery of guns, mounted on the edge of the cliff in order to protect the seaward approaches to

English Harbour, has long since been removed. From the large open space around which the guns were once positioned there is a splendid view of the whole of the south-eastern coast. Immediately below the gun platform to the east is **Indian Creek**, which contains the remains of one of the first and most important sites inhabited by the Arawaks. Further to the east are the prominent buildings of the **St James's Club** on the northern and eastern sides of Mamora Bay. Still further eastwards is the expanse of Willoughby Bay, with a line of breakers showing up the reefs across its entrance. On a clear day the outline of the French island of Guadeloupe can be seen over forty miles away to the south.

The right-hand road from the half-buried cannon leads to **Fort Shirley**. This was named after General Sir Thomas Shirley, who was Governor of the Leeward Islands in Antigua from 1781 to 1791. During this period most of the fortifications above English Harbour were built. The fort consisted of the usual parade ground and officers' quarters, together with a hospital, canteen, signal station and of course a battery of guns. The ordnance building which was behind the gun emplacement has been converted into a restaurant, and instead of guns the gun platform now supports picnic tables. These overlook English Harbour from a height of nearly five hundred feet. The view is undoubtedly one of the finest and most-photographed in the Caribbean, and from this viewpoint it is easy to appreciate the excellence of the harbour and the importance of the Dockyard to the Royal Navy of two hundred years ago. From the same place Montserrat can be seen on most days, just over thirty miles away to the south-west. Redonda, further round to the west and about forty miles away, can also be seen in the right conditions of visibility.

For those not content to sit at one of the outdoor tables and enjoy the view, within a few minutes' walk are the ruins of the military hospital. These are above **Nanton Point**, the southernmost tip of the island. Between the hospital and the rest of the fort there is a cemetery in a small valley. The various memorials and tombstones with inscriptions that are still legible show that yellow-fever and other tropical illnesses were the main dangers faced by soldiers in the West Indies in the 18th and 19th centuries. That the next greatest danger to health was the competence of the military physicians of the day is surely borne out by the proximity of the cemetery to the hospital.

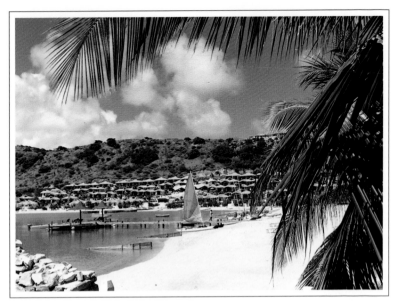

St James's Club (MICHAEL BOURNE)

Clarence House

Standing on a slope overlooking the inner part of English Harbour, and off to the left from the road leading from Shirley Heights back to English Harbour Town, is **Clarence House**. This is the official country residence of the Governor-General, although not often used as such. The house is a very fine example of the Georgian style of architecture adapted for the climate of the West Indies. When the Governor-General is not in residence it is opened to the public, and a visit is recommended. It was built in 1787 for the use of Prince William Henry, Duke of Clarence (later King William IV) who was then serving in the Royal Navy, and in command of a ship on the Leeward Islands Station. The house is still furnished and decorated very much in the style of the period. Both inside and out it appears much as it did when it was built.

Beach at Isaac Point (opposite)(CHRIS HUXLEY)

Nelson's Dockyard

After having seen English Harbour both from Shirley Heights and the garden of Clarence House, one cannot fail to appreciate its excellence as a harbour, nor to understand why a Naval Dockyard was built there. The value of the harbour as a safe refuge from hurricanes was recognised from the beginning, but it was not until the start of the 18th century that it was used regularly by Naval ships. Fort Berkeley at the end of the narrow peninsula which forms the western entrance point was built by 1704, and by 1728 a small dockyard called St Helena had been constructed on the eastern side between Commissioners Bay and Freemans Bay. The present dockyard, which is the group of buildings and wharves on the western side, on Middle Ground, was started in

The Admiral's House in Nelson's Dockyard at English Harbour (ANNE BOLT)

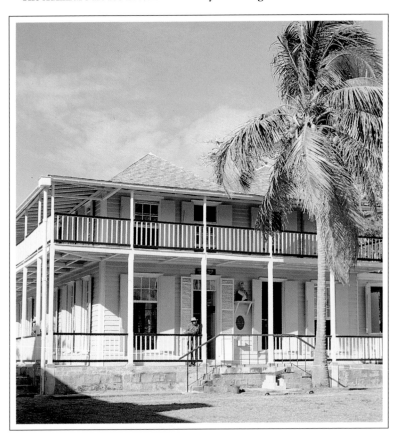

1743. Its development continued at intervals for another sixty years or so after that.

The Dockyard is now always referred to as **'Nelson's Dockyard'**, although the famous British admiral was in no way responsible for its inception or development. His only connection with Antigua was while he was captain of a ship stationed in the Leeward Islands between 1784 and 1787. During this period he spent a considerable amount of time in English Harbour. From his letters he appears to have hated it, calling it a 'vile spot' and 'this infernal hole'. Throughout his time on the Leeward Islands Station Nelson seems to have had a special dislike of Antigua and its people. 'I am not very popular with the people,' he wrote. 'They have never visited me, and I have not set foot in any house since I have been on the station ...'.

That the Dockyard should now be named after someone who not only had nothing to do with its founding, but actually detested the place, could be considered to be more than a little unjust. Nelson was not singled out for association with it much before the late 1950s but, as English Harbour developed into a prime tourist attraction during the next decade, his name became linked with what he called the 'infernal hole' from then on. It was given official sanction in the early 1980s with the creation of the Nelson's Dockyard National Park. This is by far the largest of the areas designated as such by the National Parks Authority, and embraces the whole of Shirley Heights as well as English Harbour.

The Dockyard is approached along the road through **English Harbour Town** which skirts the eastern side of Falmouth Harbour. Having crossed the isthmus the road ends at the Dockyard gate. Cars are not allowed inside but ample parking space is provided near a long, low building which houses a bank, post office and many souvenir stalls. By walking along a track which runs outside the Dockyard wall, starting near the main gate, it is possible to reach the ruins of **Fort Berkeley**. This ten-minute stroll, if taken before looking at the Dockyard itself, will complete the overall look at English Harbour and its defences. It also provides close-up views of boats entering and leaving, much as they have been doing in different forms for the past three hundred years or more.

Inside the Dockyard there is a small museum with contents equally as varied and capricious as those in the St John's museum,

Yachts at Nelson's Dockyard (overleaf) (MICHAEL BOURNE)

but naturally orientated towards the sea and the Royal Navy. It is housed in an elegant, two-storied building known as the **Admiral's House** – in another attempt to link Nelson with the Dockyard; in fact it was built 50 years after his death.

The military garrison left Antigua in 1854, but the Royal Navy continued to use the Dockyard for another thirty-five years before it was abandoned in 1889. By that time the majority of naval vessels were too big to use the harbour and the Dockyard facilities were much too limited. In 1906 it was transferred to the Government of Antigua and from then on fell into complete disrepair. It was saved from total destruction only by the formation in 1951 of the Society of the Friends of English Harbour. This was founded by the then Governor, Sir Kenneth Blackburne, who recognised the historical importance of the Dockyard as well as the role English Harbour could play as a yachting centre. Funds were collected internationally to restore many of the buildings and in 1961 the Dockyard was 're-opened' very much in its present form.

Since then English Harbour has developed into one of the finest yacht harbours in the Caribbean. It has most of the facilities needed by yachtsmen either in the Dockyard buildings or within walking distance of them. The revenue derived from the yachting industry goes in part to continue the historical renovation and preservation work. While the two activities are not totally compatible, the needs of modern yachts being what they are, a very reasonable balance has been achieved. The yachts at anchor or alongside the wharves, together with the activity going on in and around many of the buildings, add greatly to the ambience of the Dockyard. It is busier now, and particularly so during the cruising season, than ever it was during its days as a Naval Base. It is only right that Mrs Lanaghan should have the last word:

The dockyard presents a fine and noble appearance; and ...
everything seems to be conducted in the best possible manner; while
the yard itself is kept so beautifully clean, that a walk through it
affords real pleasure.

Bat's Cave and Bethesda

After touring Shirley Heights and the Dockyard the return to St John's can be made by a road running eastwards from the village of Cobbs Cross, heading towards the St James's Club on Mamora Bay. About a mile from the village a track to the south leads to a large fenced compound, once the site of an American tracking station and more latterly a medical school. This enclosure contains one of the island's least-visited natural attractions, always referred to as **Bat's Cave**. It is in fact a system of caves of which, according to Mrs Lanaghan, 'The only known occupants are bats, which breed there in immense numbers, and often attain the size of a common pigeon' and which, she goes on to say, 'In former times … was a great place of concealment for the tribes of erratic Caribs, when visiting Antigua on their predatory excursions; and tradition still points it out as the scene of a barbarous carousal among that wild and savage race …'. Before visiting the cave, for which a guide, flashlights and stout footwear are recommended, permission will have to be obtained from the current occupants of the compound.

The main road back to St John's follows the western coast of Willoughby Bay, winding through some pleasant scenery to the village of **Bethesda**. While the village today is no different from a dozen others in Antigua, Bethesda holds a special place in the history of the island. It grew up around the first school in the island, and possibly within the British West Indies generally, which taught slaves. This was opened in 1813 by a Mr and Mrs Thwaites of English Harbour Town, who gave it the Biblical name for a house of mercy. After emancipation in 1834 houses began to be built around the schoolroom, and the community emerged as one of the first 'free villages'.

Although the site of the original school has long since been lost, the site of a rather more recent event in Antiguan history is still very much to be seen about a quarter of a mile to the north of the village. It was at a meeting there, held under the large, lone tamarind tree which stands beside the road, that a sizeable number of sugar estate workers took a decision in 1951 to strike for increased pay, and to hold out regardless of the hardship they would have to endure. In the end, after nearly a year of civil unrest, strikes, strike-breaking and military intervention, they were awarded a considerable increase in pay. The large boulder near the tree was positioned there later to symbolise their determination, and to commemorate those amongst them who were imprisoned during the period of strife.

From Bethesda the road leads around the eastern side of the Potworks reservoir and so back to St John's.

SCENIC ANTIGUA

FORT
BARRINGTON

DEEP BAY

ST JOHN'S

FIVE
ISLANDS
VILLAGE

*THE
FLASHES*

Hawks
Bill
Rock

Maiden Island

Five Island Harbour

HERMITAGE BAY

Pearns
Point

Five
Islands

JENNINGS

*GREEN
CASTLE
HILL
565 ft* ▲

BUCKLEYS

JOLLY
HARBOUR

EMANUEL

BENDALS
BODY

POND'S ROAD

*LIGNUMVITAE
BAY*

BOLANS

*BOGGY
PEAK
1319 ft* ▲

SWETES

JOHN HUGHES

*DARK
WOOD*

*SHEKERLEY
MOUNTAINS*

CADES BAY

*FIG TREE
HILL*

Pelican Island

URLINGS

Johnsons Point

*CADES
BAY*

OLD ROAD

Cades Reef

*CARLISLE
BAY*

Old Road Bluff

| 0 | 1 | 2 | 3 |

Miles

| 12 |
Scenic Antigua

The south-western part of Antigua, with its steep-sided hills, picturesque villages and easily accessible, undeveloped coastline, is the most scenic portion of the island. A circular tour of this region is possible, starting and ending in St John's. It is recommended that this be taken in a clockwise direction, leaving the city by the All Saints Road.

Buckleys, Swetes and Bendals

Half way between St John's and All Saints the road divides. The right-hand fork runs southwards to the village of **Buckleys**. From there it runs along the crest of a ridge for about two miles to the village of **Swetes**. To the south-west there is a most attractive valley, with several small dams forming reservoirs which descend to the north-west. There is a road through this valley (which has no official name, although the road itself is referred to locally as 'Body Ponds' Road') beginning at the village of **Bendals**, a mile and a half to the west of Buckleys. This road provides an alternative way of reaching Swetes, but is only motorable in a cross-country vehicle.

Fig Tree Hill and Old Road

From Swetes the road is taken which leads to the west and directly into the hills. It rises and falls steeply through the village of John Hughes, meanders around **Fig Tree Hill**, and then descends to Old Road, the oldest settlement in the island. Of this part of the tour around Fig Tree Hill the indefatigable Mrs Lanaghan wrote:

... no description I have ever heard of it has sufficiently set forth its beauty: Upon one side of the road is a deep ravine, whose irregular descent is hidden by trees of every description, which cover it to the bottom, and again ascend upon the opposite bank, until they reach the top of the neighbouring mountain; on the other side are sloping hills, carpeted with the gayest emerald. This beautiful hill takes its name from several large fig-trees which grow around ...

The large fig trees are not much in evidence today but otherwise the description is perfect.

From John Hughes village it is possible to walk along a very pleasant forest trail to **Wallings Reservoir** about half a mile to the south. Construction of the dam and spillway started in 1890, but took another ten years to complete. The woods in this area not only contain some of Antigua's rarest trees, but also provides a suitable habitat for some of the island's rarer bird life.

As the road descends from John Hughes to Old Road the country becomes more open; extensive pastures are dotted with some truly enormous mango trees on one side, and small banana groves on the other. Nearer to the coast are some large coconut plantations and more extensive banana groves.

Old Road lies around the head of Carlisle Bay, and acquired its name from the fact that, for the original settlers of 1632, the bay offered a safe anchorage or 'road' (a common 17th century term for a sheltered anchorage) for their ships. Presumably, once Falmouth Harbour and then St John's Harbour started to be used the importance of Carlisle Bay decreased, and it became the 'old road'. This name then stuck to the settlement which had grown up there. Similar villages with the same name, now some distance from the main port, are found in St Kitts and Montserrat.

The village, which boasts the oldest church in Antigua, is very small and used to be very quiet. It is now situated between a large hotel at the head of the bay and another equally large hotel on a narrow headland to the west. The former, which is on a superb beach, has been designed around a series of tennis courts. The latter, which occupies the whole of the headland with a beach on either side, also has a tennis court complex in which annual professional tournaments are played.

Boggy Peak

From Old Road the road follows the coast all the way around the south-western part of the island. At **Cades Bay**, about two miles from the village, there are several large fields of pineapples under cultivation. These are of the 'Antigua Black' variety, so called because when young the fruit is distinctly dark in colour. It is smaller than most types grown commercially, but makes up for that in being particularly sweet. Since 1994 it has been designated the National Fruit.

The pineapples are grown in a small valley at the foot of the Shekerley Mountains, and the road running northwards through this valley leads to the summit of **Boggy Peak**, the highest point of the island. A microwave communication station occupies the whole of the summit behind a substantial fence. Because of the bushes and trees which grow up to this it is impossible to see anything of the views without entering the station. As this is not manned constantly anyone who wishes to avoid a disappointing climb must make prior arrangements to enter it. This can be done through the head office of Cable & Wireless at Clare Hall on the eastern outskirts of St John's (telephone 480-4000). The summit is about two and a half miles from the main road. It can only be reached by walking or in a vehicle with four wheel drive. Although the road is well-surfaced for most of its length it is extremely steep in places.

Morris Bay near Curtain Bluff in the south of the island (ANNE BOLT)

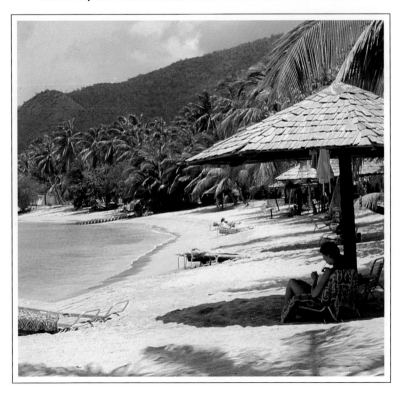

A visit to the top of Boggy Peak is strongly recommended. From it, at just over 1300 feet above sea level, the whole of Antigua (with the exception of small areas hidden by the nearer hills to the south-west and south-east) can be seen. At the same time, with reasonable conditions of visibility, the islands of Guadeloupe, Montserrat, Redonda, Nevis, St Kitts and Barbuda can also be seen quite clearly.

The west coast

From Boggy Peak the full extent of **Cades Reef**, off the coast immediately to the south, can be determined. Further views of the reef, and of the island of Montserrat on the horizon, are obtained from the main road as it rounds Johnsons Point between the villages of Urlings and Crab Hill. Just north of the latter is the splendid beach of Picarts Bay (always known locally as **'Dark Wood'**). This has plenty of shady trees and an adjacent beach bar. Another two miles on is Lignumvitae Bay, its mile-long beach dominated by one of the largest hotels on the island. Immediately to the north is **Jolly Harbour**, with a large marina and boatyard, surrounded by waterfront houses, stores, restaurants, an 18-hole golf course and recreation facilities of all kinds, and all created in an area which until the mid-1980s was nothing but a huge salt pond. The entrance to the harbour is in **Mosquito Cove**, to the south of **Pearns Point** which is the westernmost point of Antigua. This can only be reached along a rough track from the village of Jennings. This track leads to Hermitage Bay on the southern side of **Five Islands Harbour**, from where it is possible to walk to Pearns Point. The actual 'five islands' are rocks just off the point, while the harbour named after them is nothing but a large bay, as yet completely undeveloped, with a small islet, Maiden Island, in the middle.

Green Castle Hill

For anyone who enjoys hill-climbing there is a third hill, ranking after Boggy Peak and Monks Hill, which is worth visiting for the view from the top. This is **Green Castle Hill**, which stands by itself at the northern end of the mountainous south-western region. It is about a mile inland from the main road between Jennings and St John's, and about the same distance to the west of the village of Emanuel. A stone quarry is worked on one side of the hill. The track leading to the top, and which is easy to follow, starts near the gates of a brick factory associated with the quarry. The climb is relatively easy and takes about thirty to forty-five minutes, depending on the age and fitness of the climber. From the summit the view to the north is magnificent – and much better than the fairly low elevation of 565 feet and the hill's unprepossessing appearance from the road might lead one to believe.

The ashes of Lord Baldwin, who was Governor of the Leeward Islands from 1947 to 1949, are interred under a large stone plaque at one end of the summit. He helped to bring about much-needed changes in the social life of Antigua during his short tenure of office, and is remembered with affection by many of the older citizens. That this affection was returned is borne out by the words on the plaque, 'He loved the people of these islands'.

On the south and west sides of the hill near the top are some rock pillars and large boulders. As these are in vaguely circular or semi-circular formations they have acquired the reputation of being megaliths set up, as a current tourist brochure would have it, 'by human hands for the worship of the Sun God and the Moon Goddess'. As the pre-Columbian inhabitants of the island practised a form of Nature-worship, with gods of minute proportions, this seems highly unlikely. There is no record of megaliths or their like in any other West Indian island, so it is difficult to believe that Antigua was once inhabited by a race capable of, or indeed wishing to, erect stone columns weighing many tons on top of a hill. The 'megaliths' are undoubtedly of natural formation, of more interest to the geologist than the archaeologist. Green Castle Hill is still worth climbing nevertheless.

Hawk's Bill Rock, Deep Bay and Sandy Island

The peninsula forming the northern side of Five Islands Harbour is joined to the rest of the island by a narrow isthmus, separating St John's Harbour from the large marshy area called The Flashes to the south. The road over the isthmus, which leaves St John's via a causeway across the inner part of the harbour, leads to Five Islands Village in the middle of the peninsula. From the village there is easy access

View over Nelson's Dockyard and English Harbour from Shirley Heights
(overleaf) (MICHAEL BOURNE)

to the bays and beaches of the west coast. **Hawk's Bill Bay**, to the south, takes its name from the rock offshore which looks very much like the head of a hawksbill turtle, a species common in Antigua waters. Both this bay and the adjacent **Galley Bay** are each the site of an attractive hotel.

Deep Bay, to the north, is similar in size and shape to Half Moon Bay on the opposite coast. Until the mid-1980s it was completely un-developed, accessible only by sea or along a very bumpy track, with a magnificent, shaded beach and an ambience which had to be sampled to be believed. Today the beach is dominated by the highest building and the second-largest hotel on the island, and the bay is overlooked by a variety of other tourist accommodation and condo-minium developments. Fortunately the water remains as limpid, warm and blue as it always was. The wreck of a barque, the *Andes*, lies in the entrance to the bay. It sank there in 1905 while attempts were being made to unload a cargo of barrels of pitch, some of which had caught fire. It can be seen quite clearly below the surface and is much visited by divers and snorkelers.

Directly to the west of Deep Bay, about two and a half miles off-shore, is **Sandy Island**. This is only a few feet high and, apart from one or two bushes and a navigation light, is deserted. Just to the south-west of it is Weymouth Reef. This was named after the British frigate HMS *Weymouth* which was wrecked there in 1745. The wreck which can be seen there today is an Antiguan coaster. As if trying to demonstrate that there had been no advance in navigational compe-tence in the intervening 239 years, this went aground in exactly the same place in 1984.

Fort Barrington

The northern side of Deep Bay is formed by **Goat Hill**, which is the site of the fort built to protect the outer entrance to St John's Harbour. The hill was fortified from the earliest days of the settlement and has seen more action than any other fort in the island (which of course, for anyone who has read so far, is not saying a great deal ...). It was the first place captured by the French when they occupied Antigua from November 1666 until July 1667. The present fortifications were not built until 1779. They were named **Fort Barrington** in honour of the British admiral who had captured the island of St Lucia from the French the year before. Needless to say,

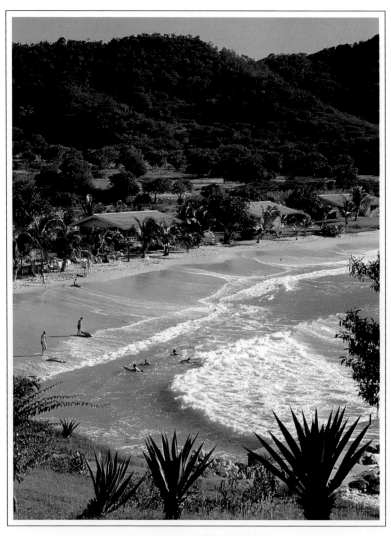

Surf riding at Hawk's Bill Beach. The small rollers make it ideal for beginners (ANNE BOLT)

once it had been built the fort saw no enemy action. After the end of the Napoleonic wars it became little more than a signal station, signalling the approach of ships to another station on Rat Island in the inner harbour.

The fort is reached by a track which winds up Goat Hill from the northern end of the beach in Deep Bay. About halfway up it passes a

Fort Barrington (CHRIS HUXLEY)

small abandoned building. This had nothing to do with the fort but was erected much later. It used to house equipment connected with an underwater telephone cable which terminated in Deep Bay many years ago. The climb is easy and takes about fifteen minutes. It is well worthwhile and provides a most satisfactory closure of a traverse of the island begun at Fort James, a mile away on the opposite side of the harbour.

| 13 |
Barbuda

Barbuda cannot be seen from Antigua, unless a special effort to see it is made by climbing Boggy Peak or some other hill with a view to the north. On the other hand, Antigua can be seen clearly from Barbuda under most conditions of visibility. This situation well sums up the relationship between the two islands. Barbuda has always been a 'poor relation' of Antigua: Antiguans are unaware of its existence for most of the time, while Barbudans – who depend on Antigua for almost their every need – must be reminded frequently of their dependency.

Formation

Barbuda is about seventy square miles in extent if the large lagoon on the western side is included in the total area. Two-thirds of the island consists of an almost flat plain raised only a few feet above sea level. The other third, known as The Highlands, is a flat tableland which has a maximum height of 128 feet. The whole island is limestone and represents a coral reef which was raised above the sea in two successive stages. The Highlands form steep cliffs on the eastern, windward, side; otherwise the whole island is devoid of any natural features which can be identified from seaward. The island has even less rainfall than Antigua, and there are no streams or lakes. Fortunately underground water is found in reasonable quantities and is obtained from wells. Virtually the whole coastline is fringed with coral reefs. Throughout its history Barbuda has been an exceptionally dangerous hazard to shipping.

History

The history of Barbuda is unlike that of any other West Indian island. Very little is known about its discovery, reconnaissance and early European settlement. Even the origin of its name is obscure. The Spanish certainly knew of its existence in the early 16th century, but the first recorded attempt at settling was made by an Englishman in 1628. This failed because of attacks by Caribs and because the island

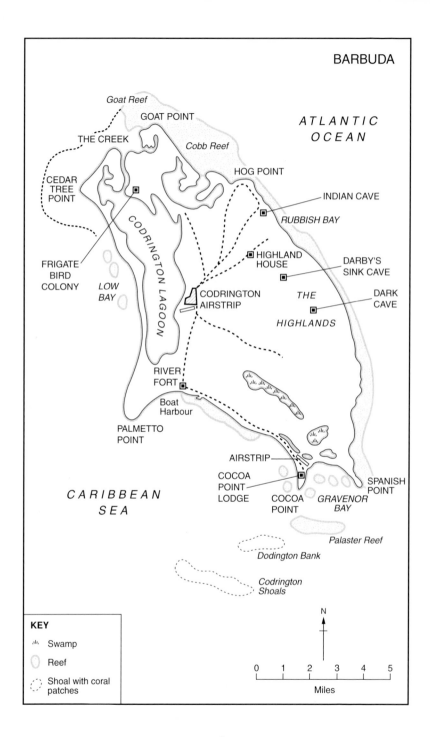

BARBUDA

Goat Reef

GOAT POINT

THE CREEK

Cobb Reef

ATLANTIC OCEAN

HOG POINT

CEDAR TREE POINT

INDIAN CAVE

RUBBISH BAY

HIGHLAND HOUSE

DARBY'S SINK CAVE

FRIGATE BIRD COLONY

LOW BAY

CODRINGTON LAGOON

CODRINGTON AIRSTRIP

THE

DARK CAVE

HIGHLANDS

RIVER FORT

Boat Harbour

PALMETTO POINT

AIRSTRIP

COCOA POINT LODGE

COCOA POINT

GRAVENOR BAY

SPANISH POINT

CARIBBEAN SEA

Palaster Reef

Dodington Bank

Codrington Shoals

N

KEY

ᶶ Swamp

〇 Reef

⟨⟩ Shoal with coral patches

0   1   2   3   4   5

Miles

126

was 'so barren'. The true history begins later in the 17th century when two other Englishmen, Christopher and John Codrington, leased the whole island from the British Crown for a peppercorn rent variously recorded as 'one Fat Sheep (if demanded)', 'one sufficient Able horse', a turtle or a buck.

Because of the indifferent soil and poor rainfall the plantation system was never developed in Barbuda. Consequently its population was unlike that of Antigua or any other plantation island. Slaves were imported by the Codringtons to raise crops and to look after cattle and other animals which were also imported. By the middle of the 18th century the mainstay of the economy was game and livestock. About two hundred slaves grew ground provisions, fished, caught turtles, cut firewood and from time to time salvaged wrecks. None of the Codrington family lived in the island permanently, and for most of the time the slaves were only casually supervised by one or two white overseers. With the freedom to grow their own provisions, with access to a great amount of livestock, and living in a dry healthy climate, the slaves enjoyed much better circumstances than those in the plantation islands.

It is a widely held belief that the large stature of many Barbudans is due to the Codringtons having used the island as a slave-breeding 'nursery'. This has been proved conclusively to be a myth, based on a mis-reading of a fragment of the documentary history of the Codrington family. Any genetic tendency towards great height and build is far more likely to be due to generations of Barbudans having enjoyed an abundance of protein from fish and livestock, while living relatively stress-free lives in a salubrious climate.

By all accounts emancipation in 1834 made little difference to the way of life or standard of living in Barbuda. The Barbudans showed much unwillingness to leave the island as slaves – faced with the prospect of work on a plantation in Antigua or elsewhere – and just as little inclination to leave once they were free. Those who did leave after 1834 were, in the main, forced to do so because no employment was offered to them on what was still a private estate. For those that remained, perhaps five hundred in all, life continued much as before.

The Codrington family continued to lease the island until as late as 1870, although Barbuda had been formally annexed to Antigua ten years earlier. After the Codringtons, others tried to 'govern by lease', without any success, until the end of the century. In 1903 the island was declared to be a Crown Estate and the authorities in Antigua

The village of Codrington (TONY AND JENNY MESTON)

were ordered to run it as such. The position of Warden was established and this official effectively administered the island for the next three-quarters of a century. In 1976 the Warden was replaced by the Barbuda Council. This body has no less than nine elected and two *ex officio* members, with sufficient powers to make the island virtually self governing. While it would be inappropriate, to say the least, to describe Barbuda as the Athens of the Caribbean, the relatively enormous size of this Council (with an elector-elected ratio of about seventy to one) means that the internal affairs of the island are conducted in a fashion approaching the Athenian ideal, and emulated in few other parts of the world. Whether of course the island's affairs are handled any more efficiently than they were in the hands of the solitary Warden, is something about which the six hundred or so registered voters probably have six hundred or more different views.

Economy

The economy of Barbuda, which after emancipation had depended to a large extent on the 'wrecking' industry and subsistence farming, today depends on fishing, subsistence farming, tourism and, as in Antigua, the 'hidden factor'. There are probably at least six times as many Barbudans living abroad as on the island. Their remittances form a substantial part of the total income. Two hundred years ago the island had one village called, not surprisingly, Codrington, and about three hundred acres under cultivation. The rest of the island was wild and overgrown with bush, in which roamed large numbers of sheep, goats, cattle, horses, pigs, mules and deer. And this is very much as the island remains today, with perhaps slightly fewer acres under cultivation and the animal population severely reduced. Codrington remains the only village, still housing the entire population of probably no more than a thousand. The modern additions consist of little more than two air-strips (one near the village and the other near the island's largest beach hotel in the south-east), a small, shallow boat harbour on the south coast, and perhaps a hundred motor vehicles. There is also an electricity generating plant and a small cottage hospital with a resident doctor.

Places of interest

In spite of the apparent lack of change, or possibly because of the air of timelessness, Barbuda does have its attractions. This is particularly so for those interested in simple pleasures and pastoral activities. For those who enjoy walking, horse riding, bird-watching, shelling and beachcombing, caving, camping, or just observing animal and plant life, Barbuda has much to offer. For others who want to indulge in less peaceful activities it also provides facilities for deer-hunting, duck-shooting and deep sea fishing.

The beaches are even better than those of Antigua. The ones on the south and west coasts are each several miles in length, and for most of the time utterly deserted. The small beaches on the north-eastern side (about four miles from Codrington) between the two geographic features with the unfortunate names of **Rubbish Bay** and **Hog Point** are equally fine, and hold an added attraction. Facing a three thousand mile expanse of ocean, these beaches receive flotsam originating anywhere in the North Atlantic as well as from Western Europe and West Africa. They provide some of the best beach-combing in the Caribbean. Offshore, enormous stretches of coral reef surround the island on three sides. With their abundance of marine life and the remains of several centuries worth of wrecks, they provide plenty of interest for the snorkeling or diving enthusiast.

As is to be expected in an island composed of limestone, Barbuda has numerous caves and the surface of The Highlands is littered with sink holes. **Darby's Sink Cave**, about three and a half miles north-east of Codrington, is the largest of these and probably the most interesting natural physical feature of the island. It is over a hundred yards in diameter and around seventy feet deep, with a reasonably easy descent to the bottom. The vegetation growing inside it is extremely lush with many tall trees and palms, ferns and lianas, and resembles a miniature tropical rain forest. One side of the hole has been greatly undercut and stalagmites up to eight feet in height have formed under the overhang.

Dark Cave, about two miles to the south, is a true cave with a narrow entrance from a shallow sink hole leading into a vast cavern containing pools of water. These were probably a source of fresh water for the prehistoric inhabitants of Barbuda, if the various artifacts which have been discovered near the cave entrance are anything to go by. They have been found in more recent times to be the habitat of several rare species of crustacea, including an unusual blind shrimp.

Far more impressive prehistoric remains, including petroglyphs, have been discovered at **Indian Cave** on the north-east coast. This is in fact a series of interconnected caverns entered through a small hole in the low cliff, which may well have been inhabited in pre-Columbian times.

At present the entire cave system of The Highlands remains to be thoroughly explored and properly mapped, and so ought to appeal to any visitor interested in speleology or potholing. The island's major attraction, however, is not underground but very much in the air. This is the **Frigate Bird Nature Reserve** in the mangrove swamp at the northern end of Codrington Lagoon, which is inhabited by around 4000 adult Magnificent Frigatebirds (*Fregata magnificens*), making it probably the largest such nesting site in the world. The birds, each of which has a wing-span of eight feet and a body weight of about three pounds, fully live up to their name and their vast, noisy rookery is well worth visiting. This is easily arranged by boat from Codrington Village.

It is not surprising, considering its peculiar history, that Barbuda has very few historic sites. Evidence has been found here and there of prehistoric occupation, but nothing remains that is of interest to anyone other than the professional or committed amateur archaeologist. Of the various historic structures scattered around the island only two warrant the visitor making the effort to view them. The ruins of **Highland House**, the Codrington family's residence near the highest part of the island, are worth visiting. They are on the north-western shoulder of The Highlands, about three miles from Codrington. The house was built around 1750, but as it was never occupied permanently it remained standing for no more than fifty or sixty years. Today all that remain are the floors and lower walls, and a large cistern, almost entirely overgrown. Perhaps the biggest attraction of a visit is the wonderful view of the island which can be obtained in every direction except to the south.

What is popularly called **'River Fort'** is the most impressive structure on the island. This is a Martello Tower and a raised gun platform situated on the south coast overlooking what used to be the main landing place, called The River. The reason for this choice of name is unclear; there never has been a river here or anywhere else in Barbuda. The fort was probably built in the early part of the 19th century when this type of fortification (modelled on a tower built on Cape Mortella in Corsica which proved exceptionally difficult to capture during the Napoleonic wars) became popular in British military engineering circles. It has extremely thick walls and the whole structure, considering the size and importance of Barbuda, was built on a monumental scale. Like many similar structures still found around the coasts of England, River Fort never saw or heard a shot fired in anger. Probably its most useful function, which continues to the present, was to act as a conspicuous landmark for vessels approaching from the south. It is about three miles from Codrington, and reached by the main road out of the village.

Visitors should beware of making too much of **'The Castle'** shown on maps of the island near Spanish Point in the south-east. This is a misnomer for the ruins of a small stone lookout and storage building. It was probably built in the 18th century but has long since fallen into disrepair. Similarly, the ruins of another building at the base of **Gun Shop Cliff** to the east of Highland House have nothing at all to do with the siting or manufacturing of guns. This structure was erected in the late 19th century as part of a short-lived phosphate mining operation, which took place inside one of the caves which penetrate the cliffs in this area.

Travel arrangements

Having mentioned some of the island's attractions it has to be pointed out that there is very little to be found in the way of facilities, support or provisions for any sort of outdoor activity requiring specialist equipment – be it a tent, an air bottle, or even a torch or a map. This may well add to Barbuda's attraction for the visitor who wants to indulge in some form of activity other than swimming, sunbathing and snorkeling.

Coco Point Lodge and Gravenor Bay (TONY AND JENNY MESTON)

Much of the, for example, speleologist's or scuba-diver's satisfaction probably stems from having to rely mainly on his own planning, resources and initiative while indulging in his particular pastime. But, special equipment and facilities apart, the speleologist, scuba-diver or anyone else intending to pay a visit should arrange the visit through a travel agent in Antigua. Everyone has to arrive in Antigua first in any case. There are no flights to Barbuda from anywhere else in the world. There are several agents in St John's who specialise in arranging such visits. A one-day conducted tour is available at short notice, but longer stays can be organised to suit individual requirements. Barbuda is linked by telephone to Antigua and an internal telephone system was introduced in 1986. There is no public transport but enough vehicles are available for rent to enable visitors to tour the island. Accommodation in Codrington is limited to a couple of small hotels, a few cottages and one or two apartments. Elsewhere on the island are two exclusive beach hotels, one of which has its own airstrip and operates its own air service for guests between Antigua and Barbuda. The scheduled public air service between the two islands (with a flight time of about twenty minutes) uses the landing strip at Codrington.

| 14 |
Redonda

The third and by far the smallest part of the State of Antigua and
Barbuda is the rocky, uninhabited island of Redonda, just over thirty
miles to the south-west of Antigua. It is roughly halfway between
Montserrat and Nevis, and considerably less than twenty miles from
either. With steep cliffs all around, it rises to nearly 1000 feet above
the sea. It is waterless, treeless, barren and uninviting, if not distinctly
forbidding, in appearance.

History

The history of the island belies its present unprepossessing appearance. Although known to the Caribs as Ocanamunru, and most likely
used by them as a convenient waystation or resting place during a
voyage across that part of the Caribbean, it did not enter recorded
history until 1493. It was sighted by Columbus on the same day that
he discovered Antigua, and he gave it the more melodious name of
Santa Maria la Redonda (St Mary the Round) as he passed by. The
first recorded landing took place in 1687, but it was not until well
into the 19th century that anyone, except the Montserratian fishermen
who visited from time to time to collect birds' eggs, took any interest
in it.

The search for deposits of the natural fertilizer guano, which took
place throughout the Caribbean during the 1850s, was carried out by
geologists working for mining companies in the United States. They
reached Redonda in about 1860 and shortly afterwards the island was
leased to a Baltimore firm which set up the Redonda Phosphate
Company. This interest forced the British authorities to consider the
status of the island and eventually in 1872 'the said Island of
Redonda' was transferred and annexed 'to the said Island of Antigua',
to which of course it has remained firmly fixed ever since.

Mining had begun on the island six or seven years earlier but in a
fairly half-hearted manner. As the total amount of guano was not all
that great, it is very likely that the main purpose in the early years
was to remove the surface material in order to reach what lay

beneath. This was a considerable amount of a phosphatic mineral (at first thought to be unique to Redonda and therefore known as *redondite* or *redonite*, but subsequently found to be a variety of the ore variscite) which contained peroxide of iron, alumina and phosphoric acid in sizeable quantities. Removal of this ore, because it was found in layers between beds of basalt, required constant blasting operations. These began, as might be expected, at the summit and gradually extended downwards. By 1890 much of the top had been removed and mining was confined to an area at the northern end of the island.

The work was carried out by a large gang of labourers, mostly from Montserrat, many of whom were only boys. The grown men did the drilling and blasting, by which the rock beds were broken up to expose the layers of phosphate, and the boys did the rest of the work. This consisted of gathering the loose ore (chipping it away from the rock fragments if necessary), getting rid of the tailings, and then carrying loads of up to eighty pounds in baskets to the dumping site. A bucket conveyor was then used to convey the ore down to a pontoon moored just off the coast, and into the lighters which berthed alongside it. Each loaded lighter was then hauled out to a ship anchored a little further out, where another gang of labourers transferred the ore into large buckets worked by the ship's derricks. The entire operation from start to finish was long, dangerous, incredibly dirty and unbelievably tedious. As over forty per cent of the ore was nothing but phosphoric acid it is little wonder that a visitor to Redonda in 1890 noted that the working of it 'caused much discomfort to the workmen by particles of it getting into their eyes'.

At the time this was written there were about one hundred workers on the island, living in two long sheds of the most basic design. The few skilled hands – foreman, book-keeper, blacksmith, and one or two others – lived apart in smaller but equally austere huts. They all existed on food which was just as basic as their living quarters – an unvaried diet of salt meat, bread, dried peas and sugar rationed out from supplies delivered from the USA two or three times a year. To drink they had nothing but water or 'tea' made from various dried grasses and leaves brought from Montserrat. The miners were engaged for three months at a time, worked six days a week from sunrise to sunset with one hour's rest at noon, and were each paid the equivalent of about one US dollar a day.

The amount of ore removed varied between 5000 and 7000 tons a year, and continued at this level until 1914, a royalty of 20 US cents a ton being paid to the colonial authorities in Antigua throughout. As by this time it was all being shipped to Germany, the outbreak of the First World War brought the trade to an end. Mining continued at a reduced rate throughout the war and a large stockpile was built up, but no ship ever returned to collect it. By 1918 artificial fertilizers were cheaper to produce and the market for Redonda's ore no longer existed. The accommodation and machinery gradually fell into total disrepair, the stockpile of ore eventually got washed away by the sea, the Redonda Phosphate Company relinquished its lease in 1930, and the island has been deserted ever since. Its inhabitants are now rats, crabs, a few goats and numerous seabirds. If its name is recognized in any other part of the world today it is probably as the result either of a tale concocted in 1929, or of a scheme carried out by the Antiguan Government some fifty years later.

The Kingdom of Redonda

Matthew Phipps Shiell was born in Montserrat, the island closest to Redonda, in 1865. He went to England at the age of twenty and, under the name MP Shiel, published a long series of well-received novels between 1895 and 1913. His literary reputation suffered a decline during the First World War and he wrote very little of any consequence after it had ended. When some of his earlier works were reprinted in the late 1920s he was asked to provide some biographical details for a publicity brochure. This was issued in 1929, and in it Shiel claimed:

... on my fifteenth birthday my father had me crowned King of Rodundo, a day of gala and of a great meeting of ships and people, many of them the worse for drink, the ceremony being performed by Dr. Semper, then Bishop of Antigua, whose palm daubed me with the balm of anointment ...

Regardless of the absurdity of the story (there has been no Bishop of Antigua named Dr Semper for one thing), obviously invented to add to Shiel's persona as a writer of unusual, fantastic and futuristic novels, it was accepted at face value by many of his contemporaries. He himself liked the idea so much that he not only embellished the fiction later in life, giving himself the title of 'King Felipe I', but

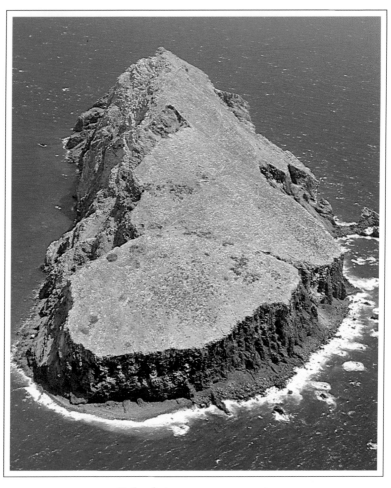

Redonda (TONY AND JENNY MESTON)

eventually bequeathed the 'kingdom' to a literary crony, who became 'King Juan I' in 1947. The make-believe continues to the present day. The reigning 'monarch', Juan II, visited Redonda in April 1979, under the supervision of a disbelieving, and possibly embarrassed, official of the Antiguan government.

Some months earlier the government, having announced the granting of 'post autonomy' to Redonda, had built a small post office near the only landing place in the south-western corner. This was manned from Monday to Friday each week for the sale of Antiguan stamps, overprinted with the word 'Redonda'. Unfortunately, as the island had been uninhabited for at least the previous fifty years, and passing seagoing customers were exceedingly few and far between, the expense involved in paying the staff and transporting them between Redonda and Antigua was hardly covered by the receipts from the sale of the stamps. The post office closed after a few months.

It is of course utterly impossible to even begin to imagine why such a preposterous scheme should ever have been contemplated by those in authority, particularly as Redonda stamps can now be bought in Antigua. A lasting result, possibly, may have been to make the name of the island as well known to stamp collectors as it is to the believers in the story of Shiel's coronation. At the same time it would be surprising if Redonda stamps were now held in any more esteem among the world's philatelists than 'King Juan II' is among the world's royal families.

Redonda resurgent

Although, as far as bird-nesting, mining, pseudo-regal shenanigans and phoney philatelic capers are concerned, Redonda has had its day, this is not to say that it is now just an uninhabited, valueless lump of real estate, or likely to remain so.

Far from it. Redonda is an integral part of the State of Antigua and Barbuda, and the sea around *all three* islands is claimed by the State as its territorial waters out to twelve miles from the coast, and out to 200 miles for the purposes of establishing the country's Exclusive Economic Zone, negotiating median lines where necessary wherever these claims conflict with those of neighbouring states. The importance of Redonda in this case, when who knows what riches may be garnered from the seabed in the years to come, can readily be appreciated from a glance at the first map in this book on page 2; Antiguans may yet live to bless the name of the colonial governor, Sir Benjamin Pine, who was responsible for the Redonda Annexation Act of March 1872.

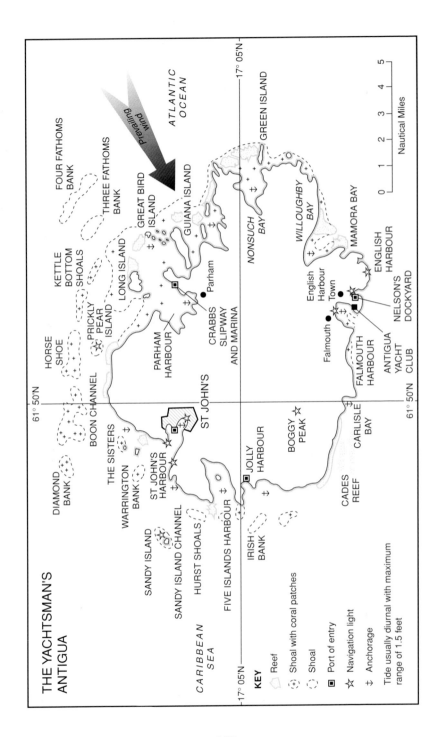

THE YACHTSMAN'S
ANTIGUA

KEY

⬡ Reef

⊕ Shoal with coral patches

⬭ Shoal

▣ Port of entry

☆ Navigation light

⚓ Anchorage

Tide usually diurnal with maximum
range of 1.5 feet

CARIBBEAN SEA

ATLANTIC OCEAN

Prevailing wind

17° 05'N

17° 05'N

61° 50'N

61° 50'N

Nautical Miles

0   1   2   3   4   5

DIAMOND BANK

SANDY ISLAND

SANDY ISLAND CHANNEL

WARRINGTON BANK

THE SISTERS

HURST SHOALS

FIVE ISLANDS HARBOUR

IRISH BANK

ST JOHN'S HARBOUR

ST JOHN'S

CADES REEF

JOLLY HARBOUR

BOGGY PEAK

CARLISLE BAY

HORSE SHOE

BOON CHANNEL

PRICKLY PEAR ISLAND

KETTLE BOTTOM SHOALS

LONG ISLAND

PARHAM HARBOUR

CRABBS SLIPWAY AND MARINA

Parham

FOUR FATHOMS BANK

THREE FATHOMS BANK

GREAT BIRD ISLAND

GUIANA ISLAND

NONSUCH BAY

GREEN ISLAND

WILLOUGHBY BAY

MAMORA BAY

ENGLISH HARBOUR

NELSON'S DOCKYARD

English Harbour Town

Falmouth

FALMOUTH HARBOUR

ANTIGUA YACHT CLUB

138

|15|
Sailing in Antigua and Barbuda

No guide to Antigua and Barbuda could be complete without some information on the islands' attractions and facilities for visiting yachtsmen. English Harbour has been a favourite port of call for ocean-going yachts since the end of the Second World War, but the true potential of the waters around the islands only began to be realised from the mid-1960s. Since then sailing in general, and ocean cruising in particular, have increased enormously in popularity. In 1960 it is doubtful if more than a hundred yachts visited Antigua in a year. By 1970 English Harbour alone was recording more than six hundred arrivals each year, and by 1990 the figure had risen to over four thousand. The services available for yachtsmen increased accordingly, and today Antigua has some of the best yachting facilities in the Caribbean.

The start of the race (TROPICAL STUDIOS)

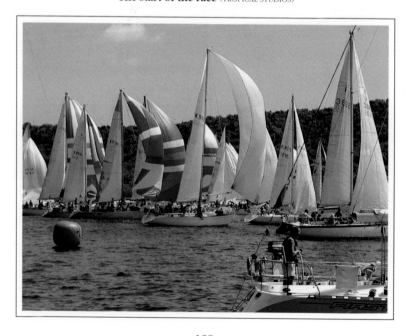

Antigua is directly on the traditional trade wind sailing route from Europe to the West Indies. It is one of the prime landfalls, especially for boats making for the Pacific through the Panama Canal. It is in the middle of the Leeward Islands, within sight of Guadeloupe, Montserrat and Nevis, and so provides a good base for cruising in that area. The weather conditions during the main cruising season from mid-November to mid-May are generally ideal. The trade wind blows from between north-east and south-east at between ten and twenty knots. Fog and gales are unknown. There is no tidal range to speak of, and the ocean current flows in a steady westerly direction at an average rate of about fifteen nautical miles a day. While the inshore waters around both Antigua and Barbuda are littered with hazards in the form of coral heads, patches and reefs, there are few which cannot be seen clearly from a boat under normal light conditions. There are sufficient stretches of open and enclosed water, with passages and anchorages of every kind, to provide enjoyable sailing for everyone from the most inexperienced weekend sailor to the most travelled sunburnt shellback.

Entry formalities

The skipper of any yacht visiting Antigua must complete a Port Authority Clearance Form and produce clearance papers from his last port of call. Each member of the crew must have a valid passport or, in the case of US or Canadian citizens, some other official proof of identity. The Immigration and Customs officials are by now well used to dealing with yachtsmen, whom they expect to obey the rules and to follow the correct procedures. A crew member is not allowed to transfer to another yacht unless the boat to which he is moving is about to leave. Anyone leaving a yacht for any other reason must have a valid airline ticket to another destination, which it is the skipper's responsibility to provide. Medical drugs and firearms must be declared. Every boat in the waters of the State must carry a valid cruising permit, issued for one month and renewable. Outward clearance is normally given only on the day of departure, after payment of the appropriate harbour dues.

Ports of entry

To facilitate the entry of yachts there are now four ports of entry in Antigua. There is also one in Barbuda, but before going there a yacht must be cleared in Antigua and the necessary cruising permit obtained.

St John's Harbour Although the Deep Water Port is solely for the use of commercial shipping, the inner harbour between the dredged turning basin and the Treasury Pier offers an excellent anchorage for yachts. There are no fees payable for using this anchorage. St John's provides by far the widest range of shopping at the cheapest prices, particularly for fresh fruit and vegetables. Fresh water, fuel and ice are all easy to obtain. There are no repair, maintenance or alongside berthing facilities.

Crabbs Slipway and Marina This is a privately owned concern on the western side of Crabbs Peninsula on the north coast. It consists of a boat yard with a fifty-ton travel lift, general maintenance facilities and alongside berths for about thirty boats. There is also a chandlery, laundry, restaurant, gift shop, post office and showers. There are also some small 'efficiency apartments' and storage rooms. The marina houses a 'bareboat' yacht chartering operation. Parham, the nearest village and from where there is a bus service into St John's, is about two miles away.

Jolly Harbour This is a large and artificially created harbour on the west coast, entered through Mosquito Cove. The facilities available include a large marina capable of handling vessels up to 260 feet in length, a boat yard with a seventy-ton travel lift, a chandlery, and a full range of dockside services.

English Harbour This is the main port of entry for yachts, developed over the years to provide every service and facility needed by their owners and skippers. Alongside berths are available at the Dockyard Quay and there is good anchorage throughout the harbour. Between November and May the harbour is very busy and it may be difficult sometimes to find room to anchor safely. Within the dockyard there are showers, lockers, a sailmaker, a marine electronics workshop, gift shops and eating places. Postal, banking and overseas telephone services are available in a large building just outside the dockyard gate. Between this building and English Harbour Town there are more eating places, groceries, repair shops and a laundry. English Harbour is the centre in Antigua for yacht chartering, and a considerable number of boats, with or without crews, are available for every type of sailing vacation or expedition.

The facilities of the dockyard and its environs are equally accessible to yachts using **Falmouth Harbour**, whose facilities have been developed considerably in recent years. It is now the preferred harbour for larger vessels, including the many floating gin palaces resembling miniature cruise liners which now grace the maritime scene. Falmouth Harbour is not a separate port of entry, but shares customs and immigration facilities with English Harbour.

It is appropriate here to add a word of caution. While it is impossible to dispute the primacy of English Harbour's facilities and attractions for yachtsmen, it is equally impossible to consider it in any way representative of the remainder of Antigua. The way and pace of life, the casual dress (and sometimes equally casual behaviour), and the general standard of living of most of the visiting yachtsmen, are not common to the rest of the island. These factors, combined with the activities of the disproportionate number of non-nationals who live and work in the area, give English Harbour a special and very different ambience. Yachting and sailing are not pastimes which appeal to, or are within the reach of, more than a tiny minority of Antiguans. In and around English Harbour Antiguans, and particularly black Antiguans, remain in the background filling subordinate positions. The visiting yachtsman who throughout his stay keeps his boat in English Harbour or Falmouth Harbour, will not on his departure be able to claim with any great conviction that he has seen Antigua or knows much about the people – any more than the vacationer who spends all his time in and around his hotel.

Cruising

The coastline of Antigua, if that of the off-lying islands is included, is well over ninety miles in length. It affords intriguing problems of navigation and seamanship, splendid sailing with superb views, dozens of secluded anchorages, and plenty of landing places. While the island has possibly more than its fair share of coral reefs these present little danger – provided that the proper seamanlike precautions are taken. Those some distance off the coast protect the shoreline and ensure reasonably calm conditions in the bays and inshore passages. The reefs are also largely responsible for the white sandy beaches which add to the attraction of most of the coves which contain the best anchorages.

It goes without saying that it is dangerous to sail around the island without up-to-date charts and pilotage information. Great Britain remains the charting authority for all of the former British colonies in the Caribbean. British charts of Antigua (upon which those published by any other country are based) provide the most authentic representation of the coastline and inshore waters. Charts produced by commercial publishers, based on the official ones and purporting to show additional information, should be treated with some reserve. The 'new' details are often of dubious authenticity or of little practical value to the stranger entering Antiguan waters for the first time. The use of larger scales to show the same information charted on the official charts at a smaller scale in no way improves the accuracy of commercial 'yachting' charts. Of more value are the various yachting guides and handbooks which are available. These give detailed information about the facilities available in each port of entry, together with sailing directions for the more popular cruising areas and anchorages. It is still necessary to recognise that, by virtue of the way these books are compiled and the length of time they remain in print, they will contain much that is outdated, misleading or totally bogus. The yachtsman who will get the most satisfaction and enjoyment from cruising in Antiguan waters is the one who uses such publications merely to supplement his own judgement, experience and capability.

Compared with many other islands in the eastern Caribbean, Antigua has a reasonable number of navigational aids in the form of lights, buoys, leading marks and a radio direction-finding beacon. Although there are leading lights marking the entrances into St John's, Falmouth and English harbours, it is not recommended that any of these be entered at night, unless in an emergency. The waters inside each harbour are too encumbered with natural and man-made hazards to permit safe manoeuvring in the dark.

While in Antiguan waters, regardless of the time of year, all professional yachtsmen will monitor local weather forecasts as a matter of course. The season for cruising in the Caribbean is between November and May, because this is the period during which hurricanes are least likely. However records show that a severe storm can occur in any month of the year – the 'hurricane season' from July to October being only the period when they are most likely. The possibility of such a storm hitting Antigua in, say, December or May is extremely remote. Nevertheless, the yacht owner or skipper who has a contingency plan ready to put into effect at any time during his stay in Antiguan waters will be the one who enjoys the greatest peace of mind.

Barbuda

As a cruising area the waters of Barbuda are not recommended for the novice. To begin with, although the island is only about twenty-five nautical miles north of Antigua it is not that easy to find. Most of it is only a few feet above sea level and it is necessary to approach within two or three miles before anything is seen. The North Equatorial Current which flows across the bank between the two islands has a rate which is unpredictable from season to season. If insufficient allowance is made for the current the west coast of Barbuda can be missed completely; if too much allowance is made a boat can end up amidst the reefs off the south-east coast. The only two features of navigational significance are the Martello tower near the south-west corner and Coco Point Lodge, the hotel on Cocoa Point in the south-east. It is essential to plan to make a landfall around midday with the sun as high overhead as possible. All the reefs can then be seen. The waters between the two islands are fished extensively, and well sprinkled with fishermens' floats. These can be made of plastic, glass, fibreglass or wood, and they are often difficult to see from any great distance. They provide another good reason for making the crossing only in daylight.

Most yachts use **Gravenor Bay**, between Cocoa Point and Spanish Point in the south-east, as an anchorage. This provides plenty of shelter, excellent fishing and snorkeling, and ready access to the wild eastern coast of the island. **Palaster Reef**, about two miles offshore to the south of the bay, is a protected area. No fishing or interference with the reef or its marine life is allowed. This reef is only one of many all around the island which have been responsible for the large number of wrecks recorded in Barbuda's history. The various yachting guides make great play with this, and give the impression that many of the wrecks are readily seen when diving or snorkeling. Unfortunately this is not the case. While the names and circumstances of many losses are recorded, the positions in which they went aground or sank are known only very approximately. Any map or chart giving precise positions of named wrecks will, regrettably, be found to be quite bogus. Anyone keen on underwater exploration may well come across some evidence of a wreck, but it is most unlikely that any identification will be possible.

Codrington village on the eastern side of the lagoon is not normally visited by yachts. The only entrance to the lagoon is through a tortuous shallow channel at the northern end. In any case Codrington has no facilities or services for yachts. The attractions of Barbuda are mentioned in Chapter 13, and many will appeal to yachtsmen as much as to the general sightseer or tourist. Indeed yachtsmen form a significant proportion of the total of all visitors to the island each year. For the skipper and crew who really want to 'get away from it all' – to have a calm anchorage and miles of deserted white beach all to themselves, and to be able to swim in water totally free from the flotsam and debris of modern civilisation – Barbuda is *the* place. But, like anyone else indulging in a pastime in Barbuda which requires specialist gear and facilities, the crew of a yacht must be entirely self-sufficient. The sagacious skipper will be ever conscious that an incident such as a grounding – which would be serious enough in Antigua where there are rescue, salvage and repair facilities available – may well mean total disaster off Barbuda, where there are none of these facilities.

Redonda

A landing on Redonda is possible only with favourable sea conditions. There is nowhere that even the smallest boat can lie alongside and the only possible anchorage, off the south-western corner, is very exposed. Once ashore there is nothing to be seen without first scrambling four or five hundred feet up a very steep couloir. Most of the remains of the phosphate workings, including ruined buildings and abandoned machinery, are to be found at the top on the only reasonably flat area at the south of the island.

Windsurfing

The normal weather and sea conditions make the inshore waters of Antigua ideal for board sailing. In recent years this sport has become firmly established. There are now windsurfer sailing schools attached to the larger hotels all around the island. Various board sailing events are held each year, including the national championships over courses off the north coast, and a regatta in Dickenson Bay which attracts participants with every degree of skill. With all the right conditions for beginners along the leeward side of the island, and the exciting wind and sea conditions off the less sheltered coasts which appeal to the more professional, Antigua has much to offer all windsurfing enthusiasts.

Waterskiing (CHRIS HUXLEY)

Antigua Sailing Week

Each year since 1968 the Antigua Hotel Association has organised a special programme of yacht races during the last week in April. This event has now become one of the finest ocean racing events in the world. Each year it attracts more and more entrants. It is an international event with yachts from perhaps twenty different countries racing in eight different classes under the International Yacht Racing Rules. The programme consists of five races spread over seven days. All the racing is extremely competitive but Sailing Week has an enviable reputation for putting the accent on 'fair sailing' and the pleasure of taking part in such splendid sea and weather conditions.

The mid-week 'lay day' is given over to more light-hearted events centred on the Antigua Yacht Club in Falmouth Harbour. These include a single-handed race, a water carnival, a nautical tug-of-war and a rubber raft race. The final day of Sailing Week is also devoted to fun and games, at the Dockyard in English Harbour. There the activities attract not only the racing crews and visiting yachtsmen, but also the general public. The main attraction is the non-mariners' race,